THE Virtual Reference Librarian's Handbook

Anne Grodzins Lipow

Library Solutions Press
Berkley

in association with

Neal-Schuman Publishers, Inc.
New York   London

Published by Neal-Schuman Publishers, Inc.
100 Varick Street
New York, NY 10013

Library of Congress Cataloging-in-Publication Data

Lipow, Anne Grodzins, 1935–
    The virtual reference librarian's handbook / Anne Grodzina Lipow.
      p. cm.
    Includes bibliographical rederences and index.
    ISBN 1–55570–445–X (alk. paper)
    1. electronic reference services (Libraries)–Handbooks, manuals, etc. I. Title.

Z711.45 .L57 2002
025.5'2--dc21

                                                                    2002029581

Contents

CHAPTER FIVE:
Update Your Library's Policies

CHAPTER SIX:
Make Your Virtual Reference Desk a Comfortable Place

List of Figures

Quick Locator of Exercises and Checklists

Foreword
by Clifford Lynch

In 1993—yes, *1993*, I had to get out my copy and check because I was having some trouble believing it—Anne Lipow kindly asked me to author a brief preface for a book she had written with her colleagues Roy Tennant and John Ober titled *Crossing the Internet Threshold*. This book—actually more of a self-instruction manual and trainer's guide—was a remarkable, and prescient, piece of work that introduced a generation of working librarians to the Internet and, at least as important, helped those librarians introduce the Internet to the general public. Anne, Roy, and John weren't the first people to write about how to use the Internet, by any means, but they were the first to make it real, accessible, and practical for a large number of people in libraries, both through their book and through the workshops that incubated and complemented the book.

The first edition of *Crossing the Internet Threshold* was written in an era before the Internet really surfaced in the public's consciousness and before the Web became the face of the Internet for most people. A reader of the 1993 edition today who had not grown up with the Internet would be puzzled—as if the book was describing some unfamiliar alternate network to the one they know. The Internet in 2002 is a very different place, an almost unrecognizably different place, than the Internet of 1993. Part of the real achievement of the book was in recognizing early that the Internet, though still evolving and unsatisfactory, would be important for libraries and librarians, and to the users they serve. The book described the tools available at the time, dispassionately and pragmatically discussed their strengths and weaknesses, and did not try to pick winners, offer definitive answers, or predict overly specific futures prematurely. It brought its readers into the evolutionary developments as participants and gave them the basic survival skills to live on the Internet and to grow along with the Internet. Those skills have naturally changed over time. The first edition of *Crossing the Internet Threshold* included about two pages on the Web and considerable discussion of systems such as Gopher, which will be unfamiliar to most people who arrived on the Internet in the latter part of the 1990s. The 1993 edition was written before Mosaic appeared. (For those who don't remember Mosaic any more than they remember Gopher, it was the predecessor to Netscape and represented the first widely deployed graphical browser for the Web.) Subsequent editions evolved along with the Internet and did, naturally, give more coverage to the Web, including Mosaic and its successors.

Crossing the Internet Threshold was—deservedly—a massive success and a deeply influential contribution. Since its first publication, it has gone through several English editions and has been translated into a mind-boggling number of other languages. It made a difference for librarians across the globe. And I can't help but believe that it played a significant, though largely unacknowledged, role in educating the library-using public about the Internet as well.

I dwell on the contributions of *Crossing the Internet Threshold* here not just to impress you with Anne's credentials but because I think it provides a helpful context in understanding Anne's current book and why this book, too, is likely to be important and worth your time.

You hold in your hands the first edition of *The Virtual Reference Librarian's Handbook*, which is about virtual reference. Perhaps more accurately, it invites and challenges librarians to reconceptualize and transform libraries into network-based *service* organizations, as opposed to simply hosts for networked information resources or facilitators of access to such resources. As such, it takes the next step—and it's a giant next step—beyond crossing the Internet threshold, and beyond all the good work that libraries have done to become network information sources as well as pathways to information accessible on the Internet.

In a real sense, this new book takes us back to the original conceptualization of the Internet as a medium and a mechanism for communication and community, and not just for providing access to information, the role that has been so heavily emphasized in the commercialization of the Internet over the last few years and in the effort to narrowly cast network users simply as information "consumers." *The Virtual Reference Librarian's Handbook* invites consideration of how libraries and librarians should be part of the flows of communication and the construction of communities.

These questions framed here are timely and important. They speak to the current debate about how libraries go beyond being physical places and help us think about the libraries of the near future, which will typically exist both in physical and network-based spheres. They also ask about how we will harness new technologies such as recommender systems and personalization, as well as a growing toolbox of methods for computer-mediated interpersonal interaction, to re-create social information finding and filtering systems in the networked world, and the role that libraries may play here.

There has been a lengthy and often less-than-helpful discussion over the past decade about "digital libraries" and how these relate to existing libraries as organizations that usually have a locus in physical space. Anne avoids these conundrums. This is not a book about the theory or engineering of digital libraries, but rather a book about how existing libraries have been extending their collections, their organizational mandates, and, more recently, their service offerings into the network world. The focus is practical and pragmatic.

This is a book that is really about questions, about the process of asking questions and challenging assumptions in a constructive, analytical, and thoughtful way, about developing new and broader visions for libraries. All the right questions are here—with a particularly refreshing and welcome emphasis on the needs and expectations of both a new generation of library users and a changing population of current and former library users, and what these imply for a rethinking of library services. But while you'll find the book's questions accompanied by a good snapshot of the developing standards, best practices, and relevant technologies, you won't find all the answers. Nobody knows what these answers are yet, and some of them are likely to be a long time in coming. Rather than claiming to give you answers we don't have, and that are likely to be very different from one organization to another, Anne's book invites the reader to become part of a process of learning and of finding and sharing answers.

It would have been much easier to write *Crossing the Internet Threshold* in, say, 1998, when the technology was more mature. But it would not have been nearly as valuable for a community of librarians who, as early as 1993, needed to be prepared to lead, rethink what they were doing, and guide and support their user communities rather than follow behind them as the Internet transformed information access. *The Virtual Reference Librarian's Handbook* obviously hasn't been an easy book to write either. It's risky to offer a guide to an immature and rapidly evolving technology and accompanying organizational and social practices. But that's part of what leadership is all about, and this book again invites and challenges librarians to become leaders and guides them through the process.

Another very valuable aspect of *Crossing the Internet Threshold* was that it recognized the growing technology-based divide in the early 1990s within the world of libraries. At that time we had a group of academic and research libraries that could take advantage of high-speed network connectivity (at least by the standards of the time) and what was then still very sophisticated experimental technology by virtue of their embedding in major universities. These libraries served users who also enjoyed access to this infrastructure. But there was another, much larger group of libraries that had to operate with much more constrained resources and technical capabilities—and serve user communities that had similarly constrained resources and capabilities. *Crossing the Internet Threshold* deliberately took an inclusive approach and spoke to both groups of libraries; this is one of the reasons it had such a large impact.

Today, the major universities in the United States enjoy extraordinarily high-speed connectivity through projects like Internet2, and there are exciting developments in areas such as immersive video-conferencing and collaboratories, which are predicated upon and are being refined within this environment. These new technologies have obvious applicability to the design of network-based library services such as virtual reference. Even at these perhaps 200 flagship institutions, the diversity of capabilities within the library user community—ranging from residential students with gigabit Ethernet to the pillows in their dorm rooms to faculty and staff with residential broadband connections all the way to a large group of people still on slow dial-up connections—presents an enormous challenge in designing appropriate and responsive network-based library services. Looking beyond this small group of libraries, however, we find many more libraries with moderate-speed commercial-grade Internet connections and technologies, serving user communities still primarily using dial-up connections but with a slowly growing base of residential broadband.

Anne's current work continues the commitment to be inclusive for the broad library community, recognizing that for many libraries service transformation will have to at least start to occur far in advance of the availability of expensive and complex leading-edge technologies that are found at the most advanced research universities. Effective network-based library services can, and will, be designed within the constraints of widely available commercial (commodity) connectivity and communications capabilities as mundane as instant messaging or electronic mail. Indeed one of the themes here is that the shift to network-based services, if carefully thought out, need not, should not, and ultimately must not wait for the availability of the next generations of network infrastructure and applications—though when these capabilities are available, they can be put to very effective use.

I will admit that I sometimes worry that virtual reference may be too limiting a vision, too literal a translation of the practices of physical libraries to the networked world, too much of a future glimpsed through a rear-view mirror. "Virtual reference" has a bit of an echo with concepts like "horse-less carriage" and may ultimately join the horseless carriage in the catalog of yesterday's tomorrows. I find myself wondering whether it may be more productive to think more broadly about network-based library services and library presence in evolving network-based communities. But it's a place to start, and we often first have to position new developments by analogy to existing technologies and services before we can really understand them in their own right. While Anne does use the rhetoric of virtual reference, I believe she pushes us to avoid overly literal translations and urges us to think hard about the deeper issues of how best to serve user communities in the digital world and to reconceptualize library services for this environment. And, as with *Crossing the Internet Threshold*, much of the message here is about getting librarians to join a community concerned with the projection of library services in the digital environment, to develop skills for survival and participation, and to position them to grow and learn as members of that community. This book will help readers become part of the definition and shaping of this new suite of services, whatever they are ultimately called.

I have had the privilege of serving as the Director of the Coalition for Networked Information since 1997. My organization is devoted to enhancing scholarship and intellectual productivity through the use of advanced networking and information technology. From this perspective, I am thrilled to see this handbook become available to help guide libraries in reconceptualizing services and relationships to their user communities in the networked information environment. Surely, this is as good a case study as one could hope to find of the potential for advanced networking and information technology to truly be harnessed in the service of scholarship and intellectual productivity. I invite and urge you to explore the emerging world of networked-based library services and join in the adventure of shaping them. Anne's work is a fine starting point to launch your participation in this collective journey of discovery.

Dr. Lynch is the Director of the Coalition for Networked Information. He is regarded as one of the most important thinkers and innovators observing the trends of librarianship, higher education, and Internet technology. For more on Dr. Lynch see www.cni.org/staff/clifford_index.html.

Preface

Clicks and Mortar

The Virtual Reference Librarian's Handbook is a practical guide for librarians and administrators who are somewhere along the path to providing virtual reference service. Perhaps you are only wondering about it. Possibly you are about to take the virtual plunge, or maybe you recently began a service and are working on ironing out the wrinkles. Whichever, you'll find here a lot you can put to use immediately. In addition, since providing a virtual reference service leads to pressures for other services, this handbook is also intended to help you think through the larger implications of providing a point-of-need reference service for your distant clientele.

While this handbook gives unconditional support to the development of virtual reference services, nothing in it should be construed as an argument against the "library as place." On the contrary, if anyone ever doubted the value of the physical library, they need only be reminded of the enormous rise in walk-in traffic in the weeks following the infamous events of September 11, 2001. People needed reliable information; they wanted to acquire whole areas of new knowledge systematically; and they wanted to be among other people who were there for the same reason: to be in unambiguously trustworthy surroundings. So adults came to the library.

Young people continue to come to the physical library as well. The children's room in any public library is as popular as any place where children frequent. Parents from all backgrounds actively encourage this participation. Those with limited budgets want their children to have access to the cutting-edge services offered at their local library. Those with greater incomes (even those parents who indulge their children with the latest computerized learning programs and speediest Internet access at home) want only the best for their children, and make sure their children go to the library regularly. In short, when adults want reliable information and the best reading materials for themselves and their children, they go to the library.

The futuristic Cerritos Public Library (Cerritos, Calif.) building, which opened its doors in 2002, is sure to be filled to overflowing with walk-in traffic, including enthusiastic repeat users, for some time to come. It aptly calls itself the "experience library": it is full of interesting spaces and displays that invite you—indeed inspire you—to want to learn more, read more, know more, experience more. (For more information about this library, go to http://library.ci.cerritos.ca.us.)

While the physical library is still very much a place, use patterns have changed dramatically. Thanks to the Internet, we now recognize that much of the information people need may not be so critical that going to the physical library or the reference desk to ensure its reliability is considered necessary. Searchers are usually willing to trust their gut feeling about whether to accept or reject information found quickly via a search engine scouring the Internet. It is understandable that many regard the convenience of ordering a book via an online bookstore a better use of their time than searching the collection of their local library. Also, we know that many, if not most, people using the Internet stations in the library are not actually engaged in the traditional library activities of reading for pleasure or acquiring new information. It is just as likely that they are conducting a home business, monitoring their financial portfolio, conversing in a chat room, or managing their e-mail.

The Virtual Reference Librarian's Handbook focuses on those aspects of library reference service that address the information and reading needs of those in the community who are finding more convenient, though perhaps not as good, alternatives to using the library. How do we reach these "invisible" people? You may quickly discover that by implementing some of the ideas in this handbook, not only do you reach them with reference assistance but you soon begin to think about other traditional services you could be making available to them. This book, then, is also intended as an opening argument for the imperative of developing an entire cyberbranch of your library.

How to Use This Book

The book is arranged in three parts:

Part 1, "Making the Decision to Go Virtual," provides the context within which to think about virtual reference. Chapter One, "Discover the Benefits and Confront the Problems of Virtual Reference," and Chapter Two, "Get Yourself in the Virtual Frame of Mind," will guide you through a step-by-step assessment and planning process. If you are on the fence about launching a virtual reference service, if you are not sure such a service is right for your library, read through this section and conduct the enlightening self-assessment, "Causes of Questions at the Reference Desk: A Survey," available in the Virtual Reference Support Materials section in the last part of the book. In Chapter Three, "Shop Wisely for Software," you will match your needs with the current software possibilities to ensure that the system you choose is right for your service and your budget.

Part 2, "Moving to the Virtual Reference Desk," is designed to help you implement or refine your service. The next three chapters explore the nitty-gritty of providing a virtual reference service. Chapter Four, "Transfer What You Know to What You Do," provides exercises that give you practice in using the new skills required in the chat environment. Chapters Five and Six, "Update Your Library's Policies" and "Make Your Virtual Reference Desk a Comfortable Place," present a structure for developing new library policies related to the service and then offer guidelines for designing your service's Web space. When you are ready for hands-on work, go through this section.

Part 3, "Building a Lively Service," is about marketing and publicizing virtual reference services. Chapter Seven, "Market and Publicize the Service in Old and New Ways," shows you how to stay in touch with your clientele's changing needs and preferences, then accommodate those needs by re-evaluating your existing services and making the right changes. It also offers constructive tips for ways to make your service known and evaluate its success. Chapter Eight, "Let the Service Sell Itself," is designed to give you the good kind of problem any service wants: too much business. Better skip this section if you prefer that your service be known only to those who happen upon it by chance!

Five appendices contain virtual reference support materials:

- The first resource is a survey you can adapt to your environment to learn the reasons people ask questions at your reference desk, and the nature of their questions.
- The second resource explains the technique of "neutral questioning" and gives examples of neutral questions.
- The third resource contains excerpts from policies and scripted messages developed by library virtual reference services, as well as a host of references to accounts of experiences as reported in the electronic and print literature.
- The fourth resource provides selected libraries' tips for communicating in a virtual reference chat transaction.
- The last resource describes an ideal training and learning environment—one that most libraries are far from achieving—to encourage you to place your virtual reference training efforts into a framework that encompasses a much larger concept of training.

Note: On the assumption that most readers will not read *The Virtual Reference Librarian's Handbook* from start to finish but instead use the Index to read about an interest of the moment, I have discussed a few ideas in more than one place, usually with some variation that is relevant at that particular point.

Finally, I like to think of this handbook as having two authors: you and me. I imagine you annotating the margins with your ideas, resulting in a kind of dialogue between the two of us. All of the forms, surveys, and exercises are reproduced on the CD-ROM in the back of this book, enabling you to customize them to suit your needs and situation. The CD-ROM also contains links to all the Web addresses cited in the book, making them accessible in two clicks of a mouse. Every effort was made to include stable sites; nevertheless, you can expect that some will have either changed their address or disappeared. So please accept my summary apology for leading you into a blind alley. I'm comforted, however, knowing that you are a member of a profession that knows how to find alternatives.

About Terminology

Digital or Virtual?

The vocabulary for these electronic reference developments is still young, so it isn't surprising that there is confusion about some of the terms we are using, in particular, whether the terms *digital reference service* and *virtual reference service* are synonymous. Some, especially library technologists, say digital reference encompasses a broad range of electronic reference activities that include creating and managing digital reference resources (digitizing paper materials, producing original digital resources that have no paper counterpart, making available such electronic resources created elsewhere, constructing FAQ files, and such) *as well as* providing personalized reference service via the Internet, whether by e-mail or chat. The National Information Standards Organization (NISO), on the other hand, is in the early stages of developing standards for "digital reference services," by which it means reference services "delivered via real-time chat or asynchronous e-mail [that] allows patrons to submit questions and receive answers via electronic means." The NISO definition is the one used in the name of the pilot phase of the Library of Congress-led global remote reference service project QuestionPoint, the successor to the Collaborative Digital Reference Service (CDRS). QuestionPoint uses both e-mail and chat technologies to deliver service. To learn more about QuestionPoint, go to www.loc.gov/rr/digiref/.

As the services in the electronic environment become more sophisticated and complex, it becomes ever more important to have precise and distinct meanings for the terms we use. Lacking an authoritative lexicon, I use the term *virtual reference service* to distinguish the narrow focus of this book—live, interactive, remote service—from the broader definitions. The term *virtual reference librarian*, then, refers to a librarian who provides point-of-need live, interactive question-handling using chat and voice software that enable synchronous communication with a distant client. E-mail and Webform reference services are forms of digital reference service but are not encompassed in virtual reference service.

Patron, Customer, or ...?

Throughout *The Virtual Reference Librarian's Handbook*, I refer to the people who use libraries as "clients." This term is the least offending word I can think of since it is often applied to people who use professional services. "Patron" is associated too easily with the person who supports a charity, or with "patronizing" as in "condescending." In this women's occupation of librarianship, we don't need more vocabulary that conveys the "servant" part of our work as public servants. "Customer," on the other hand, smacks too much of the buying side of a business transaction; using a library should not be regarded as a business transaction. "User" is a fine word from my standpoint (and I do use it when the emphasis is on utilization, such as in "Internet user" or user of a particular service). But I'm surprised at the numbers of people—librarians and clients—who conjure up images of drugs and addicts at the word, and I haven't yet figured out how to turn that into the happy notion of addicted library users.

One More Thought

Today reference librarianship is in the most exciting position it has been in since its birth over a century ago. And reference librarians are the key to the continued success of libraries. As I've heard David Lankes, founder of the annual Virtual Reference Desk Conference, say numerous times, it used to be selectors who filtered out the junk and ensured quality materials in libraries. Today it is reference librarians who are the filters. Whatever else you derive from *The Virtual Reference Librarian's Handbook*, I hope you experience this sense of being present at a revolutionary moment in our history.

Your Comments Are Welcome

If this book should someday be updated, I'd want it to include what you thought was missing, clarify what was unclear, correct what was wrong, and keep what you found helpful or expand on it. Please e-mail me your thoughts at anne@library-solutions.com (and make the subject heading something substantive, such as *A comment on your book*, so that I don't inadvertently delete it).

Acknowledgments

The credits in this book are far too few. When I am certain of the source, I attribute a specific idea to that person. In the main, however, most of my thoughts about the changing nature of reference began in some form in the creative minds of colleagues with whom I have spent many hours over many years thinking through difficult issues facing libraries or figuring out which path to take when the profession seemed to be at a crossroads. The trouble is that I have integrated their thoughts into mine to the point where I can't any longer say who exactly influenced which ideas. But I know who these colleagues are that have made me smarter, so I here acknowledge them en masse, with my deepest respect for their large ideas, farsightedness, and ability to accomplish wide-sweeping innovations.

Suzanne Calpestri	Carole Leita
Jerry Campbell	Clifford Lynch
Steve Coffman	Ethel Grodzins Romm
Sheila Creth	Anita Schiller
Richard Dougherty	Karen Schneider
Maurice (Mitch) Freedman	Steve Silberstein
Cheryl Gould	Elaine Sloan
Helen Hayes	Roy Tennant
Holly Hinman	Lou Wetherbee
Patricia Iannuzzi	Joan Frye Williams

One of the above-named people, Steve Coffman, needs to be singled out for being more than a significant influence on my thinking. Steve is the reason there is an audience for this book at all. Without Steve, virtual reference would be a long time in coming. Ever since 1992, when I conducted the first of my Rethinking Reference institutes, I have been advocating (some would say nagging) that reference librarians devote their attention to their remote constituencies. "Nice idea," "interesting," even "you're right" was the response, but nothing changed. It was Steve, joined by Susan McGlamery and Linda Crowe (the first to turn Steve's ideas about the power of networking into real systems), who triggered an overnight mushrooming of libraries eager to go virtual. With his amazing energy, his large and hearty personality, and his provocative writings and debates, Steve worked both sides of the street—on the one hand, shaping to the reference environment the technology that had been designed for commercial use, while on the other hand, pulling librarians into the virtual reference orbit. Lest a historical footnote should one day mistakenly credit LSSI (Steve's employer) with giving birth to virtual reference in libraries, let the record show that this was Steve's baby, conceived well before he joined LSSI, while a librarian in the Los Angeles County Library.

A nameless group of colleagues to whom I owe most of what I know about reference are the hundreds, probably thousands, of librarians throughout the United States, Canada, Australia, New Zealand, Denmark, and The Netherlands, from every type of library, who attended my workshops or whom I assisted with their efforts to rethink every aspect of reference service; and my co-workers at the University of California, Berkeley, Library, where I worked for three decades.

I am indebted quite specifically to the following people:

- Christine Borgman for introducing me in the early 1980s to the Einstellung Effect (Chapter Four)
- Suzanne Calpestri for the analogy of librarians to chefs (Chapter One, sidebar)
- Suzanne Calpestri and Linda Arret for explaining just how complex the reference interview can get when trying to figure out which format of a work the client needs (Chapter One, Dispelling Doubts, "Contrary evidence says don't go virtual")
- Paul Constantine for tipping me off to the new specialty in the medical profession called "hospitalist" (Chapter Two, sidebar)
- Patricia Iannuzzi for the advice about eliminating interruptible time (Chapter One, Six Approaches to Carving Out a Niche for the New Service)
- Clifford Lynch for the concept of the library learning the client as opposed to the client learning the library (Chapter Two, Think Like Your Clients Think, "Take a new look at old ideas")
- Karen Schneider, without whom I would have left out approaches 5 and 6 in Chapter One
- Bernie Sloan, whom I have unofficially dubbed "The Historian of the Virtual Reference Realm," for tirelessly collecting and sharing with the online forums information about every facet of librarians' experiences with virtual reference services
- Joan Frye Williams for many of the ideas in Chapter One about eliminating or reducing work, which she expressed in a California Library Association Conference talk, "Submerging Technologies," November 2001

Library Solutions Press is to be credited for giving its permission to reproduce or adapt sections and exercises from its loose-leaf publication *Establishing a Virtual Reference Service: VRS Training Manual*, by Anne G. Lipow and Steve Coffman (February 2001, updated August and December 2001), including an explanation of Neutral Questioning, as well as the chapter on shopping for software.

Also, for sharing their invaluable experiences, my thanks go to the many colleagues—including especially members of the electronic discussion group LiveReference, as well as subscribers to the *VRS Training Manual*—whose comments on earlier drafts of Chapter Three: Shop Wisely for Software have greatly increased the usefulness of the information in this book's revision of that chapter.

Technology maven Rod Flohr must be credited with repeatedly rescuing my sanity. When my computer misbehaved or when the software I needed to use required more than a get-by knowledge, I had only to hear his "I can handle that" to return my blood pressure to normal levels.

A big THANK YOU! goes to my persistent, yet ever-tactful editor, Michael Kelley, for not allowing the manuscript to stand as I originally submitted it. His "Why don't you try this...?" or "It might make more sense to arrange things this way...." or "This part would benefit from a more balanced approach...." was always prefaced with "This is good, but..." I shudder at the thought that the before-Michael version might have seen the light of day!

Finally, there is no succinct way to properly express my thanks and appreciation to my assistant, Charlotte Bagby. She is H.W. Fowler (master of English usage), Katharine Hepburn (as librarian in *Desk Set*), Radar (as in *MASH*), and Frederick W. Taylor (of efficiency fame) rolled into one. If there are factual or grammatical errors in this book, I can assure you that I snuck them in after Charlotte was done with the manuscript.

Part 1
Making the Decision to Go Virtual

The goal of a library, as every librarian knows, is to "get the right book to the right person at the right time." Library catalogs, embodying the principles of bibliographic description and access formulated by the great library thinkers Lubetzky, Ranganathan, and Cutter, have been organized around this lofty ideal, and reference librarians have stood ready to help when the catalogs fail. However, neither the catalogs nor the reference librarians have been able to come close to meeting the ideal. Both have been limited by Newtonian laws of time and space.

The Internet and its World Wide Web, however, have lifted those limitations, and libraries, referring to themselves as "libraries without walls," make available via the Internet their catalogs and indexing tools as well as a significant amount of the material represented in those finding aids. The location of the information seeker in relation to where the information sought is stored, at whatever time of day or night, isn't relevant; the information itself—whether in the form of full texts, moving or still images, or sounds of every variety—can be delivered to the requester in an instant. Research-level materials once available only in large metropolitan and academic libraries can now be accessed from the most far-flung rural communities.

Not surprisingly, this unprecedented access to an infinity of unorganized information has unleashed a new population of information seekers, which, in turn, has dramatically increased the need for help with finding information. Reference librarians would be the natural choice to provide this service, but since they were slow to rise to the occasion, commercial reference and information services have moved in to fill the vacuum by making themselves available round the clock via the Internet.

Today, libraries are aggressively catching up. They are asking a new question: not "How can we get our clientele to come to the library to use the wonderful services we have for them?" but "How can we bring those services to wherever our users are?" In particular, "How can the reference desk be where the users are when they have a question?" Their answer is, "By offering a virtual reference service." By moving their reference desks and themselves onto the Web, pioneering reference librarians are playing a central role in enabling their libraries to achieve the goal of getting the right information to the right person at the right time. This section, Part 1, is intended to help you grapple with the complexity of issues involved in the decision to launch a virtual reference service in your library.

Chapter One
Discover the Benefits and Confront the Problems of Virtual Reference

Three Reasons to Offer a Virtual Reference Service Now

Reason 1. You want to close the growing gap between users and the library

Libraries of all types are experiencing a noticeable change in use by their constituencies. Whether from a computer inside the library or from their homes or offices, Internet users are getting their questions answered by robotic search engines that spew out a discouraging number of irrelevant responses, and by commercial service representatives who have superficial skills and limited resources for linking the questioner with quality answers. Many, if not most people might prefer the expertise of a reference librarian, but when faced with the library's limited hours, parking difficulties, the mental picture of having to wait in line at the reference desk, and off-putting hurdles in reaching the library by telephone (not to mention less tangible barriers, such as concerns about anonymity or their eligibility to use the library), they lower their sights. Their natural tendency to accept handy mediocrity overrides their desire for quality. According to Roy Tennant, that's human nature: "At a 'good enough' point . . . it becomes too much trouble to reach the optimum for the perceived gain . . . ." (Tennant, 2001: 39) When given a choice, clients are willing to be "satisficed" rather than satisfied if to achieve the latter isn't convenient. (See sidebar "The satisficing syndrome.")

It should be no surprise, then, that point-of-need questions at the reference desk are declining and reports of a decrease in circulation of nonfiction print materials are on the rise. In many communities, as use of the Internet increases because of connectivity at the home and office, once-regular library users come to the library less often, and formerly nonlibrary users who don't have comput-

The satisficing syndrome

"Anyone who has worked at a library reference desk has seen users pleased with a quick and mediocre answer when, with a bit more time and effort, they could get a better one. It's human nature to seek that which is 'good enough' rather than the best. For many, it's a simple equation of effort vs. payback . . . . When this aspect of human nature intersects with digital libraries, we have all the makings of what I call the 'convenience catastrophe.' This catastrophe is nothing more or less than the disappearance of our print collections in the face of more easily obtained digital content. Collections that are easy to access by using a computer and an Internet connection will very frequently win out over print collections—no matter how much better and more inclusive our print collections may be. Once our clients begin to see the Internet as the answer to all or most of their questions, our sources of support will be in jeopardy. [Librarians must] meet the challenge of moving our users from satisficing to satisfying, from minimizing to maximizing . . . ." (Tennant, 2001: 39–40)

Declining walk-in traffic?

A true story: The librarian of a public library in Illinois opened its doors one morning to the usual three-deep waiting crowd. When they heard her announce that the library's Internet connection was down, but all else, including the online catalog and circulation system, were fine, they *all* turned and left. For the three days that the library was without its Internet connection, the only people who came into the library were those who had received notices to pick up the books they had reserved.

The new "problem patron"

In libraries where there are not enough Internet computers to accommodate the demand, some of these newcomers, when told their time at the computer is up, mount an escalating confrontation to resist giving up their seat. The disruptive client, not recognizing that libraries function on a principle of sharing, is motivated by a different principle: possession is nine-tenths of the law. It doesn't take many such "difficult patrons" to have a stressful impact far out of proportion to their numbers. Libraries that have installed software to manage computer scheduling say it significantly reduces the incidents of intransigent clients and they can spend more time informing this new clientele about other library services.

ers, or whose personal computers have slow connectivity, come to the library solely to use the Internet. (See sidebar "Declining walk-in traffic?") Librarians report that this new clientele tends to use the Internet not to find information but rather to check e-mail, conduct a business, visit sexually explicit sites, check stocks, play games, or participate in chat groups. (See sidebar "The new 'problem patron.'")

Motivated by these changes, libraries are forging new relationships with their clients. Throughout the United States, reference librarians marked the new millennium by placing reference desks onto the Internet. The year 2001 was when virtual reference services sprouted from a few brave libraries that in 2000 had ventured out into the unknown to hundreds of libraries offering chat-based reference service in a variety of patterns using more than two dozen software brands. They knew full well that diminished use of the in-library reference desk did not mean clients didn't have questions. They believed that their clients, if given the choice, would want the expertise of a reference librarian to assist in finding answers over those who staffed the commercial services. (See sidebar "Will clients choose a virtual library service over a commercial one?")

These libraries established virtual reference services to accomplish any one or more of the following:

- **Provide the best quality reference service to the majority of the library's clientele, including those who won't or can't come to the library.**
- **Provide handy reference service to in-library clientele from in-house Internet stations.**
- **Distribute the reference staffing load among branches.**
- **Achieve greater staff efficiency by collapsing multiple reference points within the library or library system and placing throughout the library and its branches virtual reference stations: clearly identifiable computers that link to staff at the centralized physical desk.**
- **Form a network with other libraries to share the staffing load and increase the virtual reference hours, with the goal of providing round-the-clock service.**
- **Form alliances with special libraries to improve referrals when specialized collections and their staff's expertise are called for.**

Reason 2. You can't afford to wait for the perfect technology

It will be some time, say the pundits, before video and audio technology on the Internet develop to the point of replicating the physical environment. But to wait till that day would be a mistake. A fundamental reason to establish a live, interactive Internet-based reference service now is to join the rest of the world in providing convenient access to your reference staff for clients who don't, won't, or can't come into the building. Bear in mind that for a steadily growing percentage of communities, an ever increasing portion of their lives is lived in the world at their fingertips. From their desktops or their wireless hand-held computers, they shop for anything from books to real estate, search for information on any subject, engage in conversations with people around the world, take classes, manage their money, seek a mate, check out theaters and restaurants, read today's newspaper from almost any city anywhere, store family photo albums—you name it.

Granted, those who can take advantage of new technologies are those who can afford them, a growing (as prices come down) but far smaller population than the have-nots. However, it is the have-gots who vote for and in other ways support libraries, so it is imperative to satisfy their changing information needs and expectations. Their support is what ensures the library's ability to maintain its standard of equal access to the best resources using the latest technologies for everyone.

Now, here's the rub. Along with each technological innovation that gains acceptance among significant numbers in your community comes a change in their expectation of how quickly something can be accomplished, their perception of what they can accomplish on their own vs. when to get help, and their definition of a service that can give them the help they need. It is understandable, then, why the library that doesn't have a virtual counterpart to its reference desk service might look ever more antiquated to its clients.

Or, to put it another way, whereas once the reference desk was the only place to get difficult questions answered, today your clients have many alternatives. Their world now includes easy access to search engines that keep getting smarter and are increasingly able to retrieve relevant information to complex questions in no time. In a matter of seconds, a relatively untutored Internet user can perform rather sophisticated searches using powerful tools.

For example, let's say you want help in finding information about how violence on television affects children. Also, you want to have translated a passage in an article on this subject that appeared in a French newspaper. Which strategy would you choose?

a. go to the library, check the shelves, go to a French dictionary, and ask the reference librarian for help, or

b. from your home or the library's Internet connection, do the following two tasks:

- **Go to Google (www.google.com), and enter: impact +violence +TV +children [Review the results]**

Will clients choose a virtual library service over a commercial one?

Media coverage of the Library of Congress's Collaborative Digital Reference Service (CDRS), now called QuestionPoint, a Web-based live reference service provided by librarians throughout the world, supports the belief that a library-provided reference service is viewed by most as superior to a commercial service. The newspaper *Mercury News* (San Jose, California) of March 18, 2001, said as much in its headline "Move over, Google. Make way, Yahoo! Meet Lynn, the live, online reference librarian." An informal survey conducted by CNN.com was more explicit. Along with a UPI wire service article describing CDRS that appeared on CNN's Web site on November 20, 2000, CNN.com took a "QuickVote" on the question "Will you use a library-sponsored reference Web site or stick with your usual sources?" The tally of the responses was reported as follows:

90% The library site will become my top choice.

7% I'll use it, but I'd rather stick with established sites.

3% I'm happy with what's out there already.

Whatever words you search by, Google is likely to turn up something that's acceptable to you. It may yield an overload of answers to your question, but its formula for displaying them in descending order of relevance makes it likely that if the answer to your query is anywhere in the set of retrievals, it will be among the first several entries.

- Go to AltaVista's uncomplicated Babel Fish language translator (world. altavista.com) to get the following passage translated rapidly from French to English:

"Un sondage réalisé par la American Medical Association a démontré que 75% des parents ont déjà fermé leur téléviseur ou quitté une salle de cinéma en raison du contenu trop violent du spectacle."

Babel Fish immediately responds as follows:

"A survey carried out by American Medical Association showed that 75% of the parents closed already their television set or left a movie theater because of the too violent contents of the spectacle."

We can expect the near future to provide ever better tools (Abrams, 2002). Check out, for example, some of the search engines that provide a visual display of the relationship among the retrievals or in other ways make searching more intuitive and successful, such as Teoma, WebBrain, iLor, and Kartoo.

Even closer to home is the popularity of commercial reference services. Whereas once the term *information professional* was synonymous with *librarian*, that is no longer the case. Your clients have handy access to commercial Internet-based reference services staffed by live people called wizards, guides, experts, and other such titles that express an expertise and an eagerness to help on any topic whatsoever. Some are available 24 hours a day, seven days a week. They are personable people, often hobbyists, who give quick answers. They started out answering questions free of charge but were so overwhelmed with callers that most now charge a fee. Here is a sampling of commercial Web-based reference services:

allexperts.com or expertcentral.com (free)

answers.google.com (fee varies)

liveadvice.com (fee varies)

keen.com (fee varies)

webhelp.com ($10.00 buys ten requests)

Despite fees, these services get thousands of questions a day on every conceivable subject, proving that there is a need to be filled and that librarians are not filling it.

It should be noted that these commercial services, unlike a library service, have a clear revenue objective. Their Web pages are usually replete with distracting advertising, and if you ask, "What strategy did you use to get the answer to my question?" at least one such service will reply, "Sorry, that is proprietary information." Others will provide an answer to a factual question but either withhold the source of the answer or have no other source to declare but themselves, drawing from their alleged in-depth knowledge about your topic. Their customers don't seem to realize that such practices render the information they provide suspect; or perhaps their customers don't care that there may be a commercial bias embedded in the answer.

We can't take comfort, however, that we will remain the only trustworthy source of free information. For example, in mid-2002, the Wondir Foundation, a nonprofit organization, appeared on the horizon. It was formed with the mission of eliminating "the barriers between questions and answers." It claims to be a "different kind of information service . . . to connect people who have information needs with the people and information that can help them." The service, says the Wondir Foundation's Web site (http://wondir.org), will provide free "unfettered access to relevant information." The information it provides will come from "service organizations, government agencies, libraries, universities, charities, advocates, mentors" whose mission is service as opposed to making money.

So if libraries are to coexist with these other information service providers, they need to keep pace, despite knowing that no blueprint exists for where they will be headed. One thing is certain: if that pace continues to accelerate as it has in the past, it will spawn changes in our lifetime that we can't imagine today. (See sidebar "The accelerating pace of change.")

Thus, comparing their location-based services to other, handier services their clients are experiencing, including smart search engines and live, Internet-based commercial help desks, librarians are reshaping their libraries to fit with their clients' changing definition of a helpful service.

Reason 3. You want to continue providing the best service possible

What reference librarians love most about their work is the face-to-face interaction with their clients as they help them find the information they need. So their concerns about point-of-need reference service in the chat environment, in which both parties type their conversation, are understandable. First, typing your conversation

---

The accelerating pace of change

Technologists tell us that if the pace of change continues to accelerate as it has in the last two centuries, emerging technologies will soon eliminate the keyboard and mouse (you speak and your words are written or your command is obeyed). Moore's Law, based on Intel inventor Gordon Moore's observation in the mid-1960s, asserts that computing power doubles every 18 months. If history is any guide, says Steve Jurvetson, "Moore's Law will . . . jump to a different substrate. . . . The exponential curve of computational power extends smoothly back in time to 1890, long before the invention of the semiconductor. Through five paradigm shifts, from electromechanical calculators to vacuum tube computers to the integrated circuit, the processing power that $1000 buys has doubled, on average, every two years. For the past 30 years, it has been doubling every year." (2001:39) An instance of Moore's Law is that greeting card you got that plays a song when you open it. The tiny chip in the card has more computing power than all the world's computing power in 1950!

is inefficient: it takes a lot more time to type something than to say it. Also, you need to compensate for the absence of visual and auditory cues; in written form, you must elicit from the client, as well as convey to the client, the useful information you each would otherwise get in an instant by seeing and hearing each other. Despite these obstacles, interactive chat service has a key advantage over all other methods currently in use, including face-to-face service in the library: it can provide just-in-time service to the information seeker regardless of the library's hours or the whereabouts of the client.

Think about it: A reference librarian standing behind a desk waiting for someone to say, "I can't find what I'm looking for, can you help?" might be justifiable if, like other service professionals, that librarian was the reason the person came to the library to begin with. But the library, organized on the principle of independent use, expects clients to find what's needed on their own and relegates the reference librarian working at a desk to "just in case" status. Moving the reference desk out to the Internet places the librarian where the clients are: amid the chaotic information landscape, a far better place to be as a bridge to quality information.

A study based in Scotland shows why "synchronous" service—in which both client and librarian are present at the same time, either face-to-face or using interactive conferencing technology—is superior to all other genres of reference service. (Davenport, Procter, and Goldenberg, 1997) Understanding why this is so is a two-step process. First, think about the genres of reference services and, for each, where the *service* and the *service user* are physically located in relation to each other. Figure 1–1 shows that relationship as follows:

In-library/Face-to-face	Both the service and the user are in the same place at the same time
Web-based tools	Both are in the same place at different times
Phone, Web conferencing	Each is in a different place at the same time
E-mail	Each is in a different place at different times

Then, comparing the relative value of the different service genres, Figure 1–2 shows that in-library face-to-face and conferencing are the most effective in resolving the questioner's problem in a timely manner.

This study tells us that if we could raise the "availability" score of conferencing from low to high (round the clock, accessible from anywhere there's an Internet connection), it would be the preferred

Figure 1–1 **The genres of reference service in time and space**

	TIME		PLACE
	SAME	**DIFFERENT**	
In-library Face-to Face		Web-based reference tools: • FAQs • Homemade resources • Client-centered links to other reference resources	**SAME**

Telephone Web-based conferencing:
   • Text (Chat)
   • Audio
   • Video
		E-mail	**DIFFERENT**

Figure 1–2 **Characteristics of types of reference service**

	Effectiveness (Resolution of problem)	Responsiveness (Speed of answer)	Current Availability (Accessibility of service)
In-library Face-to-face	High	High	Low
Telephone	Low-High	High	Low

Conferencing
  Text only
  Audio...
  Plus video
	
	High
	Higher
	Highest
		
		High
		Higher
		Highest
			
			Low-Medium
			Lower
			Lowest

E-mail	Medium	Low-Medium	High
FAQs, etc.	Low	Low-High	High

point of first contact; and conferencing with audio and video combined would come close to replicating the in-library/face-to-face service (whose availability score cannot be raised because of its inextricable link to time and place). E-mail might be the preferred method of follow-up.

Six Approaches to Carving Out a Niche for the New Service

You ask: How can we possibly add another service when we can barely staff the reference desk now?!

The truth? You can't. The number of hours in the day hasn't changed, so starting a virtual reference service requires that staff throughout the library work differently. Here are six ways to approach the problem.

Approach 1. Make room for new work

Against a backdrop of an updated mission, figuring out how to work differently is accomplished by examining all current functions and assigning as many as possible to one of three categories: (a) cease the function because it is no longer valued, or reduce it by shrinking its dimensions; (b) reassign the duties elsewhere; or (c) automate the function out of existence. Let's take the three alternatives one at a time.

a. Cease work or reduce other work

Candidates that will result in the elimination or reduction of work are equipment, files, and practices that require attention but are no longer effective. For example:

- Aging equipment that only one person knows how to maintain.
- Publication formats that require discontinued equipment to view or that are used by very few.
- Stand-alone computers that access particular databases. (Change to networked workstations.)
- Handwritten files. (If they contain useful information, transfer them to machine-readable form, thus making them available to other staff.)
- Interruptible time. Command respect for your work and time by not allowing yourself to be interrupted by drop-in clients when you are not on desk duty. Practice saying, "I'm busy at the moment. Let's make an appointment when I can give you my undivided attention." Or, "My schedule is booked today, but let me call the person on duty at the desk to let her know you need help now."

b. Reassign duties

This alternative requires that you redefine professional work. The finding tools we have today make it possible for paraprofessionals to catalog materials that once demanded someone with an MLS (or equivalent) degree, and to locate library materials that once required the service of the most experienced librarians. For example, until the early 1990s, the staff of interlibrary loan (ILL) departments in large research libraries were librarians, often senior librarians. This is understandable because, if a wanted publication was not found in the comprehensive multimillion-volume collections of a large research library, chances are it was either of an esoteric nature or that the citation was garbled. Obtaining the publication took clever sleuthing and considerable knowledge about the bibliographic structure of publications in different countries, different languages, and different topics. Today, with so many readily accessible choices at one's fingertips for locating publications of all types in all languages without needing to know much of the publication's formal particulars, paraprofessionals staff the ILL services, with a librarian available for the few requests that call for advanced knowledge.

Reassigning work is best done within the context of redesigning the organizational structure of the library to enable a more fluid use of staff. "Borrowing" staff from, say, technical service departments to help during the busiest reference times doesn't work well because as soon as the technical service department gets busy, it will take back the lent staff member. It is a good idea to give entirely new names to the new departments to better reflect your new organization of work. (See "Invent New Vocabulary" on page 32.)

The most creative examples of eliminating or reassigning work challenge tradition or represent out-of-the-box thinking. Libraries that have eliminated their reference desks altogether and now provide triage services at prominently placed service points staffed by highly trained library technicians have certainly challenged tradition. And libraries that are extending their staffing by joining with staff from other libraries to accomplish round-the-clock service are quite literal examples of out-of-the-box thinking.

Librarians in one-person libraries obviously have to be creative in figuring out where to reassign some work or what work can be automated. The Ironwood Branch of the Richmond Public Library in British Columbia, Canada, has transferred many traditional functions to its clients! Borrowers there check out their own materials (the special design of this service is why 85% of clients take advantage of it, as opposed to 15% in most other libraries); they fetch their own "on hold" materials from an open shelf (the books are jacketed in white paper and only the client's name is on the spine); and, on returning their materials, they sort them by dropping them into one of four slots: Adult Books, Kids' Books, Chinese Books, and CDs/Videos. You can learn about other innovative ideas this wonderful library has implemented at www.rpl.richmond. bc.ca.

c. Automate the function

This alternative has the biggest payoff in freeing staff to perform new roles. Functions that have been automated out of existence by some libraries are the following:

- *Management of traffic on computer workstations.*

  Software can enable the client to book computer stations from afar or from within the library, alert the client when the session is about to end, allow the client to take a short break without losing his seat, and cancel no-shows.
- *Circulation procedures: check-out and check-in.*

  The popularity of check-out stations rises the more strategically located they are and the better they are designed to be perceived as easy and quick to use. For checking in materials, there is radio frequency technology that can check in a full drop-in cart of returned materials without human intervention.
- *Notification to clients of overdue materials and books on hold.*

  Such notices are most effectively handled by automated telephone and e-mail messaging systems.

Approach 2. Redefine "professional" work

Reference librarians who have eliminated work they had been doing that doesn't require an advanced academic degree spend more time using their expertise appropriately, including preparing the library for what's expected next.

An entry-level reference librarian's week might look like this:

6–8 hours	Maintains office hours to be on call for accepting referrals from the information desk and for drop-in consultations.
2–6 hours	Staffs the virtual reference desk, especially the second tier, to which are sent referrals of questions requiring special subject expertise and collections.
4–6 hours	Consults with clientele one-on-one by appointment to provide in-depth assistance. Includes prep time for the consultation.
6–8 hours	Oversees and sometimes provides in-person group instruction. Includes preparation time.
6–10 hours	Works on technological solutions to instruction to be able to reach more clients where they are when they want to upgrade their information literacy and research skills.
4–6 hours	Hangs out in clients' milieu, reads their literature and bulk mailings and attends their meetings to keep up with their changing information needs and to make the librarian's work more visible.
2–4 hours	Selects reference materials in all formats.
4–6 hours	Meets with colleagues within and beyond their library to share experiences, identify problems, and consider solutions.
1–2 hours	Contributes to the profession by, for example, writing articles for publication in library journals and community media, and providing leadership in professional organizations.

The reference librarian might also engage in continuing self-education one or two days a month.

A reference service administrator might spend a token amount of time on both the physical and virtual desk (to keep abreast of changing needs and to identify and propose solutions to problems), and may contribute to collection development. However, the greatest portion of the workweek is spent thinking, planning, analyzing, experimenting, forging alliances, and meeting with staff, clients, funders, and decision makers within the library as well as those in the library's parent organization, with the goal of ensuring a thriving future for the library.

Approach 3. Create new work

Once your library has an up-to-date definition of "professional work," your job must come as close as possible to consisting exclusively of that work, and you must resist allowing other types of work to encroach on it.

Here are some new and emerging job titles or responsibilities representing professional work that focus special attention on bringing the library to the client. The underlying assumption of these positions is that a growing proportion of a library's clientele will not come to the library but would use its services if they were available at their desktops.

- Customer/community relations manager, who is concerned with addressing the needs of members of its constituencies who don't, won't, or can't come to the library (includes marketing, needs assessment and analysis, pilot projects)
- Instructional designer, information literacy programs planner, who designs and implements instructional programs that reach clients wherever they are
- Technology liaison, who works with systems staff in designing new user-friendly Web-based and other electronic services and whose goal is to put as many of the in-library services onto the Web as possible
- Special services coordinator, who develops new services, especially Web-based-services, to meet newly identified needs, including those of special-interest groups and targeted categories of clientele where they are
- Fee services developer (may be folded into services coordinator responsibilities)

Approach 4. Redesign space

If your library maintains a reference desk and you can manage the staffing, the virtual reference desk should ideally be separate from the physical desk. Librarians report the following problems with trying to work both desks from the same space:

Librarians are like master chefs

Providing less than the best tools for reference staff is like expecting a master chef, whose job is to help others with their cooking problems, to get the job done with a Coleman stove when the clients all have Wolf ranges. The chef is an expert in the chemistry and art of cooking and knows which ingredients are the best and where to get them. Imagine, then, the chef dealing with clients who have the technology but not a clue about the quality of the ingredients or how they change when heated. How would you describe the service the chef could provide? How motivated would the chef be to experiment and learn more?

- The client standing at the desk doesn't understand that you are helping another client when there is no one else around and you are seemingly only typing at a computer.
- If your virtual reference system alerts you that there is a remote client waiting for you, you must interrupt your work with the in-person client to promptly attend to the virtual client.
- Until your skills are well honed, it is likely you will be exhausted after two hours of work at a busy virtual reference desk. Adding in-person clients to your workload, as well as the distractions and interruptions that go with your working in a public space, may well result in burnout.
- To ensure similar access to resources as you have when working at the physical desk, when you are working at the virtual desk, you should ideally have a wireless hand-held computer to be able to move about the library with the virtual client.

Still, a few librarians I've spoken to prefer providing the virtual service from the physical desk. They make the very good argument that it ensures that both they and their clients perceive the two types of services as integrated. Also, one desk makes it easy to monitor the goal of giving equivalent service to both remote and walk-in users. Assess the feasibility and weigh the benefits and shortcomings of one vs. two spaces for the two services in your environment.

In my opinion, having a separate space for virtual reference at the very least should be a choice. For the times the service is provided away from the reference desk, you'll need to make a special effort to compensate for what you are losing by not having the two kinds of services in the same space. I prefer separate spaces because it doesn't work well to have two busy services in the same space, or, if you prefer, one busy service with two unique modes of operation. If you are able to manage both services from the same space, most likely one or both of those services is little used, in which case you should examine why, and work to promote the services and increase business.

Approach 5. Provide the necessary underpinnings

You should do whatever you can to help staff members do their jobs. At minimum, this task requires providing staff with the technology they need to be successful and the training to use the technology effectively. (See sidebar "Librarians are like master chefs.") In libraries, this is a generally recognized principle—except when it comes to reference. In too many libraries, for example, reference staff members share an Internet station. This situation usually occurs in libraries that have received a government or foundation grant stipulating that the money can be spent only on equipment for use by the public. This shortsightedness has two consequences:

1. Undertrained staff. The staff's ability to practice new skills and stay abreast of changes is hampered by the inaccessibility of a basic tool they are expected to know.

2. Ill-spent funds. The largest, most expensive component of a library's budget is staff salaries. If you do the math, you will find that it is far more expensive to have fewer productive staff members than it is to provide the tools they need to get the job done right. If you are going to provide a virtual reference service, at minimum, the staff should have the benefit of

- **Fast connectivity**
- **Quality workstations**
- **Appropriate software**
- **Continuous training**

Approach 6. Give the new service time to succeed

Just as you would for any new service, you will, of course, want to test your new virtual reference service with a pilot group, devise methods for correcting the bugs, and create benchmarks for evaluating its success. Expect a virtual reference service to go through more bumps and setbacks than any in-library service you've launched. Therefore, don't be discouraged, and above all, don't give up when you are not meeting your expected goals within the first three months. That's because you are using never-before-tested equipment, practices, and policies in a never-before-provided medium for your service. So have patience. Both you and your clients have a lot to learn. It may take at least a year before you know whether this service will work in your library.

Dispelling Doubts

Contrary evidence says don't go virtual

In the previous sections of this chapter, we discussed some of the forces driving change in your clients' information-seeking resources and in their relationship with the library and some reasons why a virtual reference service is a good response to these changes. You still may have doubts, though. The status quo, after all, is powerful. It provides you with plenty of evidence to stay the way you are. To eliminate your doubts, let's look at some stock reasons for why change to virtual is difficult, if not impossible, and, after examining their validity, offer a rebuttal.

Evidence: *True, we're serving fewer people at the reference desk, but we're busier than ever!*

Rebuttal: Yes, you're busy, but doing what? Chances are you are dealing with "Do you have this book?"; "Show me how to search this database"; "The computer has frozen"; "Please fix the paper jam"; "I've never used a mouse before"—requests that can be handled competently by people without a professional degree. An analysis of the questions asked at your desk, as recommended in the survey in Appendix 1 (see pages 149 to 155), should convince you that you should be doing different work than sitting at the desk passively waiting to be asked a question.

Evidence: *The questions we get at the reference desk today are far more complex than the old days, so we spend more time with each client.*

Rebuttal: It may feel as though the questions are more complex, but the evidence doesn't support this conclusion. As was always true, the resources that searchers turn to first are those they know. When their trusted strategy doesn't work, they may well conclude that finding an answer may be difficult. Even though clients may use the Internet as their first strategy, there is no reason to believe they are effective searchers. So it holds true today that the client who comes to you for help may perceive the question to be complex, but you find it easy. It is just as likely that you take longer because you haven't sufficient knowledge of Internet resources and search strategies to perform efficient searches or, because there's always the possibility that what you're looking for exists somewhere on the Internet, you don't have a sense of when to stop.

Evidence: *A growing number of resources come in multiple formats (print, CD-ROM, and Internet-based) and some even come in the same formats by different providers (publisher, aggregator). Although they may be the same work in different formats or by different producers, each version has different strengths and shortcomings. For example, the paper edition of a newspaper has obituaries, and the online version provided by the same publisher does not, but the online version published by an aggregator does! Or the client correctly cites the headline of a newspaper article in the paper edition, but that article in the newspaper's online edition has a different headline. Also, aggregators add and remove titles at will without notifying subscribers. So in addition to trying to keep up with those differences, we need to go through a lengthy interview to be sure we are recommending the appropriate version.*

Rebuttal: No argument here! As long as multiple formats and providers of a single work last, and if you are lucky enough to be able to afford all of them, you will be challenged to keep up with their differences in content, indexing, and retrievability. The trick is to apportion your day so that you spend more time keeping up with these developments and sharing what you learn with colleagues, which in turn will enable you and other staff to efficiently interview the client about what is wanted and to know which of the several versions should be consulted.

Evidence: *Our users say they love us the way we are.*

Rebuttal: Libraries always come out winners in surveys that ask respondents to assess the library as compared with other government or campus services. Librarians get pleasure out of helping others, and it shows. However, your high marks may be due to respondents' low expectations about what library services are possible. For example, if you ask, "How satisfied are you with the service(s) you receive in the library?" the response will be limited to the services you give that the respondent takes advantage of. You might get a very different answer if you asked, "How do our access and delivery services compare with those of amazon.com?" You surely will learn about any mismatch between your clients' needs and the library's services if you ask, "How often do you need material or information when the library is closed?" And you might learn about the effectiveness of your publicity campaigns if you ask, "Where else do you go when you need information?" Responses to this last question may reveal that the respondent goes elsewhere when the library should be the first choice.

Evidence: *Answers given by the dot-com reference services are far inferior to ours.*

Rebuttal 1: Maybe so, but all indications show that if their inferior answer is "good enough," the information seeker is happy enough and will look no further.

Rebuttal 1: Can you be sure your answers are superior to those of the commercial services? Research consistently shows (starting with Hernon and McClure, 1986) that reference librarians answer only 55% of the questions correctly, so there might not be much difference! Librarianship is one of the few professions that doesn't require continuing education to renew certification; therefore, it is probable that for every librarian whose record is far better than 55%, one scores much worse.

Evidence: *Commercial reference services come and go. We're always here.*

Rebuttal: Let's restate that to be more descriptive. Commercial reference services may come and go, but because they have proven to be a major point of attraction to their Web sites, new ones can be expected to replace the old ones, offering easy access and attractive enticements. To the extent they replace traditional library services, libraries will continue to exist, yes, but may find themselves marginalized, relegated to serving only the have-nots.

Evidence: *Our clientele doesn't really know what we do. If we did a better job marketing our services, users would flock to us.*

    Rebuttal: If true, why is that so? Is it because you have always been the only free information resource in your community, so the percentage of your constituency that frequented the library—avid readers, parents and their children, students with assigned readings, people gathering information for a project—was sufficient to keep the staff busy? And now that you have some competition, do you lack experience letting people know you are there and performing services they need? Under those circumstances, if you were a business, you'd soon be closed.

Evidence: *The value of the reference desk lies in the personal face-to-face interaction. All that is lost in the coldness of cyberspace.*

    Rebuttal: When the video component of interactive remote reference is better developed, there will be little difference between the physical and virtual desk from the standpoint of enabling personalized service. But in fact, in the current chat environment, to the extent that you can easily refer your client to others in your network, it may well be a superior service. You might regard chat reference service as the preliminary step before an audio and video component is a viable option. In the chat medium, you can achieve the personal touch by your choice of words and by the extra benefits you provide, such as a record of your conversation and sites visited sent to them via e-mail.

Evidence: *We can barely staff the physical desk. How can we possibly add on another?*

    Rebuttal: If you simply launch a virtual reference service without making other changes in your library, the service will be a burden, leaving you cranky and resentful, so you will put little energy into turning it into a successful business. To ensure that your virtual reference service thrives, you will need to make room for it by redesigning services and jobs throughout the library. Ideas for how to do this are discussed in "Approach 1. Make room for new work" on pages 10 to 12.

Evidence: *If it ain't broke, why fix it?*

    Rebuttal: If it ain't broke, now may be the only time you *can* fix it. Once broken (for example, plummeting use of library services, loss of support by taxpayers and other bases of funding), it may be too late to regain your status and clientele. For corroboration of this point, see "New Interpretations of Old Rules" (Barone, 1993).

"*I'm* eager to go virtual, but how to convince the others?"

You: *You're asking a lot, Anne. Even if I bought into half of it, it will be a hard sell to the rest of the staff. How do I convince the disbelievers?*

AGL: Leave the skeptics alone. If you wait for total buy-in, you'll never get anything new off the ground. The larger your organization, the longer it will take to convince everyone in it of the rightness of going in a new direction, not to mention the same direction. In fact, think about not needing to have everyone go in the same direction. Any organization that wishes to be around tomorrow must today be offering not what their customers are asking for but what they believe their customers would love to have but don't know enough to ask for. To do this, organizations must have "the ability to run *experiments in the margin* [emphasis mine], to continually explore new . . . organizational opportunities that create potential new sources of growth." (Senge, 1990: 7) What this means is that you should start small, involving only the enthusiasts, and experimenting with pilot projects for targeted audiences. Once your project is a proven plus, others will come around. Your success will also encourage others to try out their ideas. Some libraries have even established a department of experimentation; staff with ideas that have been approved for development spend part of their workweek, for a defined span of time, in this department. In that way, the library truly becomes a learning organization.

References

Abrams, Stephen. 2002. "Let's Talk About It: The Emerging Technology Future for Special Librarians." *Information Outlook* 6, no. 2 (February): 18–27.

Barone, Carole. 1993. "New Interpretations of Old Rules." *Cause/Effect* 16, no. 1 (Spring): n.p.

Davenport, Elisabeth, Rob Procter, and Ana Goldenberg. 1997. "Distributed Expertise: Remote Reference Service on a Metropolitan Area Network." *The Electronic Library* 15, no. 4 (August): 271–278.

Hernon, Peter, and Charles McClure. 1986. "Unobtrusive Reference Testing: The 55 Percent Rule." *Library Journal* 111 (15 April): 37–41.

Jurvetson, Steve. 2001. Transcending Moore's Law. In *CNET Tech News/Perspectives* [Online]. Available: http://news.cnet.com. [28 August 2002].

Senge, Peter M. 1990. The Leader's New Work: Building Learning Organizations. In *Sloan Management Review* Reprint Series 32, no. 1 (Fall): 7–23.

Tennant, Roy. 2001. "The Convenience Catastrophe." Digital Libraries column, Library Journal [Online]. Available: http://libraryjournal.reviewsnews.com/index.asp?layout=article&articleid=CA185367&. [15 December 2001].

Chapter Two
Get Yourself in the Virtual Frame of Mind

Spend Time Appreciating Your Work

The library reference desk has been around since the late 1800s, long enough that it is possible you take it for granted and haven't thought about the true value of your work. Ethnographer Bonnie Nardi's research (1998) shows that the work of reference librarians is invisible both to their clients and to themselves. When asked what you do as a reference librarian, you tend to reply, in effect, "I answer people's questions" or "I link people with the information they are seeking." Nardi concludes that what you do looks on its surface to be replaceable by software, but in fact what you do is quite complex and cannot be accomplished by computers. She calls reference librarians "information therapists" and worries that unless you begin to value the brain power that goes into your work and make your special skills known, reference librarians are in danger of becoming extinct. Because reference librarians operate within a system of people, practices, technologies, and values, Nardi believes you are part of an information ecology, within which you are a keystone species: if the reference librarian disappears, so will diversity in information resources.

Throughout this book are ideas for making your virtual service (and you) visible to and valued by others. To be sure *you* appreciate your importance, here are two basic axioms to stimulate your thinking about the value of your work.

Axiom 1. Your job is not to answer questions

If you are a reference librarian, you know that your clientele, all information seekers, share a common behavior: each one approaches you with a question. But do you know why someone goes to the trouble of seeking you out to ask a question? And why the question asked is frequently "wrong"? Every reference librarian has often experienced a client who asks a different question from the one she or she wants answered. Why do they do something so counterproductive? Unless you know the reasons, you will view your job as answering questions, a function that today can be handled by software or by people without a library degree. To understand the professional nature of your work, as well as why a virtual reference service is critical to the health of today's libraries, requires an appreciation of the object of your profession: the information seeker.

Brenda Dervin, inventor of the art of neutral questioning (NQ)—an interviewing technique that helps the reference librarian efficiently understand the client's question—and Patricia Dewdney claim there are three universal truths about information seekers (1986):

- *Situation.* Every information seeker is in the process of "sense-making." They are in the midst of a situation in which they have lost their sense of how to continue.
- *Gap.* Each is cognitively blocked and wants to become unblocked but is missing some information.
- *Use.* Information seekers know the use to which they plan to put the missing information. (The information that will fill the gap depends on how they view their situation, which, in turn, dictates how they plan to use the information to become unblocked.)

If only information seekers knew to tell you that use at the outset, there'd be no need for NQ! How their initial question is formulated often has more to do with their assumptions about how the library's resources are organized than with what they are hoping to find. Imagine these scenarios:

Scenario A. Three people ask you a different question, but they all want the same answer. For example, the three questions "Where are your books on China?"; "Can you help me locate information about cures for cancer?"; and "Where can I find information on cooking with herbs?" might be asked by three people, all of whom want recipes that use a Chinese herb that is effective in cancer treatments.

Scenario B. Three people, all blocked in very different situations, might ask the same question ("Can you help me find information about China?"), but the answer each needs might be different (one wants the history of a Chinese province; another, information about a Chinese herb; the third, the value of a collection of Chinese porcelain).

Scenario C. Three people who are blocked in the midst of the *same* situation might each view their plight differently. Imagine, for example, a situation in which a fire destroys the homes and possessions of three neighbors; each has a different sense of their situation and, therefore, a different sense of what they need to move on. Although they might all ask the same question ("Can you help me find information about insurance claims?"), the answer that will satisfy each might be different, including one that has nothing to do with insurance claims!

Figure 2-1 is a simple representation of these three scenarios.

Figure 2–1 Relationship of question asked to answer wanted

	Scenario A	Scenario B	Scenario C
The *situation* of the three information seekers →	Their situations are the same... ↓	Their situations are different... ↓	Their situations are the same... ↓
The question asked at the reference desk	yet their questions are different... ↓	yet their questions are the same ↓	yet their questions are different... ↓
The answer to the question	but the answers they need are the same.	but the answers they need are different.	and the answers they need are different.

Unless you have a method for discarding your own assumptions about what clients want based on the misassumptions implied in their questions, you will be serving the same function as a search engine. The method that ensures you give only relevant information to each one is "neutral questioning." (For practice using neutral questioning in the chat environment, see the exercises in Chapter Four, pages 65 to 68.)

In sum, your job is not to answer questions, but to eliminate blockages by filling in gaps with information relevant to the individual.

Axiom 2. There will always be a need for a human consultant to satisfy the needs of the information seeker

It's safe to say, then, that everybody is an information seeker—that is, everybody will be stuck, over and over again throughout their lives, and will consult some thing or some person to become unstuck. Whether the information seeker is successful using a non-human resource (such as a book or a search engine) to become unstuck depends on several factors, such as

- whether they picked a resource that contains or can lead to what will unblock them;
- how much they know about how the resource they are consulting is organized;
- how much they know about how to query the resource (for example, its rules of grammar, punctuation, syntax);
- how aware they are of the appropriate vocabulary to use to convey their question.

Every nonhuman information system is organized in a way that optimizes a desired level or type of retrieval, and questions must be asked of it according to some guidelines peculiar to that system. So the chances are slim that the information seeker will *always* choose the right resource *and* know its rules for querying it *and* retrieve relevant information.

Also, people vary in how they best absorb new information. Some prefer to read it, some prefer to hear it; some prefer to first ask an expert, others will ask only if all else fails. Regardless of their preferences, if the information seekers' starting strategy doesn't work, they try another. Whether as a first choice or last resort, everyone will at some time need a human consultant to become unstuck.

Remind Yourself: To Want Convenience Is Human

Discard any notions you may have that a person who wants service at 2:00 a.m. is unreasonable, or that catering to the client who wants full-text articles in printed journals delivered now is pampering a demanding person. Information seekers have always been impatient to get answers to their questions. In pre-Internet days, research showed that when looking to fill the gap of missing information, first people went to their own home bookshelves, then they telephoned a friend or colleague who was likely to know, and, probably last, they went to the library. (Van House, 1991) Once in the library, they may not ask their questions of a reference librarian, even if they cannot find the answer they're looking for on their own, because oftentimes the reference desk is out of sight, or they don't realize you can help them find what they need. (Many librarians report that the people who ask a question at the desk are those with whom they have made eye contact!) In other words, people will go first to the most likely source that is convenient. The Internet, when it is handy, is now the strategy of first choice.

The striving for the perfect information system—whatever money could buy or minds could imagine—goes back a long way in time, and its main characteristic is always its convenience. *Isaac*

Asimov's Book of Facts tells about the Persian warrior, statesman, and scholar Abdul Kassem Ismael, who "in the 10th century had a library of 117,000 volumes. On his many travels . . ., he never parted with his beloved books. They were carried about by 400 camels trained to walk in alphabetical order. His camel driver librarians could put their hands instantly on any book their master asked for." (Asimov, 1979: 215)

Or, consider L. Frank Baum's information system created in his 1920 book, *Glinda of Oz*:

> Dorothy . . . ran over to a big table on which was lying open Glinda's Great Book of Records. This Book is one of the greatest treasures in Oz and the Sorceress prizes it more highly than any of her magical possessions. . . . I do not suppose there is any magical thing in any fairyland to compare with the Record Book, on the pages of which are constantly being printed a record of every event that happens in any part of the world, at exactly the moment it happens. And the records are always truthful, although sometimes they do not give as many details as one could wish. But then, . . . the records have to be brief or even Glinda's Great Book would not hold them all. . . . (Baum, 1920: 3–4)

Even in magicland they sacrifice quality for convenience! If *convenience* governs the choice of where to go, it makes sense that information seekers are turning to the Internet. What is more convenient than information at your fingertips? And when it is a live and knowledgeable information specialist that is needed, who better than the reference librarian? Indeed, it may be that the real value of a convenient reference desk is to satisfy the clients' desire to talk to someone at their point of need, to have their questions *heard*. Most are quite willing to wait for the answer, whatever time that takes, knowing it is being worked on.

Face the Realities of Reference Desk Work

As you learned in the opening of this chapter, reference librarians tend to undervalue their work when they describe how they handle reference questions. In this section, we'll talk about their opposite tendency to overvalue their work when they describe what they actually do at the desk. (See sidebar "The real work we do vs. what we think we do.") Their account seems closer to their abstract job description than reality. Reference librarians claim to spend most of their time at the reference desk answering reference questions, but chances are that isn't so. An honest analysis of questions at the desk generally reveals that well below 50% of the questions are of

The real work we do vs. what we think we do

Reference librarians are not alone in misperceiving their work. Studies of leaders vs. managers show that corporate executives, when asked to describe how they spend their day, say that most of it goes into thinking and analyzing, articulating the company's mission and vision for the next period, and other "big picture" issues that would ensure the company's healthy future. However, when observed as they actually go through their workday, a very different picture emerges. Executives deal mostly with nitty-gritty issues: putting out fires, handling sticky personnel situations, making decisions about small expenditures, and so forth. (Kotter, 1990; Zaleznik, 1989)

the type that requires an advanced professional library degree. I know of no studies that compare the time spent on such questions to time spent on other types of questions, but it's my impression that there are no discernable differences: you can take a long time with a "nonreference" question and a minute or two with a "real" reference question, and vice versa.

In today's world of accountability, you must get a realistic handle on what you do so you can contribute constructively to discussions and decisions about the future of the library in general and reference service in particular. Jerry Campbell, noted challenger of the library status quo, calls it the "need for conceptual clarity about . . . [your] role in the context of the changing knowledge environment" and for "reliable data about the practices of reference" without which "it will be hard for us to improve how well we carry out [our mission]." (Campbell, 1993: 6–7)

In Appendix 1 is an instrument—a survey—designed to increase your awareness of the nature of questions that come to your reference desk. Of the many times I have administered it to academic and public libraries, the results have been consistent: the number of questions considered to be the type needing consultation with a reference librarian falls within the range of 14% to 46%, with most hovering between 30% and 39%. I encourage you to conduct this survey. In addition to making you more conscious of the types of questions, the results inherently provide you with the *causes* of questions that come to your desk, giving you clues about how to address those causes; that is, on the premise that every question asked at the reference desk represents the failure of the library to be obvious enough for information seekers to find what they were looking for on their own, the survey helps you develop several categories that represent the conditions that caused the questions. Armed with that information, you can proceed to eliminate or reduce the frequency of certain types of questions, simultaneously increasing the clients' skills in using the library independently and raising the percentage of true reference questions asked at the desk.

In short, to acquire a realistic picture of what causes a person to ask a question at your reference desk, conduct the survey as described in Appendix 1 (see pages 149 to 155).

Learn to Welcome Change

With the pace of change accelerating, it is understandable that the staff who do best in this climate are those comfortable with ambiguity, confusion, and uncertainty. They seem to welcome addressing new issues, trying out new ideas, and letting go of old habits to make room for new ways of doing business. If this description doesn't fit you or some of your colleagues, take the quiz in Exercise 2–1. It is intended to undermine your sense of being on solid ground, a first step toward feeling excited about change, looking forward to it, and contributing energetically to shaping it. After you complete it, tally the score and note its significance.

Exercise 2-1. **Your awareness-of-ambiguity score**

Place a mark in one of the two boxes to the left of each statement. Choose the answer that most closely reflects your views.

Mostly true	Mostly false or haven't thought about it	
❏	❏	1. In my library we aren't sure what difference the MLS (or equivalent library school degree) makes. Paraprofessionals work side by side at the reference desk with librarians and do a fine job of answering rather complex questions.
❏	❏	2. We've had informal discussions in our library about whether we should be calling ourselves something other than "librarian." We note that library schools are either closing or dropping "library" from their names. Also, with one exception, we are the only professionals who are called by the name of the building we work in, and we wonder whether that makes it harder to think about our work separate from the building. (The exception is the subcategory of doctors who are called "hospitalists"; their jobs are indeed defined by and confined to the building they work in. See sidebar "What's in a name?")
❏	❏	3. We are aware that sometimes our clients don't understand our jargon. For example, some clients don't know what "reference" or "circulation" or "serial" or "periodical" or "catalog" means. Many ask a reference question at the circulation desk.
❏	❏	4. We sometimes feel we are losing control over our collections. Approval plans and bulk purchases of serials that include some titles we don't need are undermining our selection responsibilities.
❏	❏	5. We are concerned that our expertise in the science of information retrieval is diminishing. In card catalog days, we knew how our files were organ-

---

What's in a name?

According to the National Association of Inpatient Physicians (www.naiponline.org/about/hospdef.htm), "the term 'hospitalist' refers to physicians whose practice emphasizes providing care for hospitalized patients . . . and hospitalists typically spend most or all of their work day in the hospital. . . ." (Wachter and Goldman, 1996: 514–517) The term was coined in 1996 by two doctors writing in the *New England Journal of Medicine*. Regardless of whether "librarian" was ever intended to define the information professional as one who works in a library building, that definition lies somewhere in the unconscious of many of us, including me. It emerged in a colleague's question to me and my response to her, after I had left the library where I worked and started a library consulting practice. "What's it like," she asked, "not being a librarian anymore?" To which I defensively responded, "I most certainly am a librarian!"

ized; we could correct mistakes; we could change headings. To find information today, we use smart software that keeps its functionality a trade secret. (Dorman, 2001)

❑ ❑   6. We don't have much confidence in the security of our electronic systems.

❑ ❑   7. We're not sure what all the legal and ethical issues are in relation to our users' accessing objectionable material, such as Internet sites containing sexually explicit or violent content. In fact, we don't have a good answer to parents who demand filtering software for our Internet stations. We do not want to be in the position of censuring material, and we reject filtering software because it doesn't work (for example, it prevents access to benign sites). On the other hand, we don't want kids to have access to pornography, whatever that is.

❑ ❑   8. We don't feel as though we have a good grip on copyright law as it applies to use of our licensed electronic databases.

❑ ❑   9. We are keeping our eye on e-book developments. E-books are slow in coming, but as soon as hand-held reading devices begin to approach the look and feel of a paperback book, they will catch on. It will then be possible for an online bookstore to not only sell the book at a list price but also, for a smaller price, "lend" the book for a specified number of hours or days (after which it self-destructs), or even lend chapters of a book. We should be thinking now about what the role of the library will be in such an environment.

❑ ❑   10. We aren't sure how to resolve the contradiction between our commitment to preserving our clients' privacy and our desire to provide more personalized service, which requires maintaining records of their use of materials, reading tastes, reference questions, and so forth.

❑ ❑   11. Again on the question of privacy, in these times when national security is an issue, when the greater good may be at stake, we have begun to think about whether we have a responsibility to report an information seeker with suspicious motives to the authorities.

❑ ❑   12. The quality of reference service is uneven in our library because continuing education and training is not a high enough priority. For example, some of us learned the Internet by the seat of our pants, so our search strategies at the reference desk are too often based on haphazard guesses. In fact, a librarian may have had no more formal training than what was learned years ago in library school, so newer resources and tools that would answer the question are not used.

YOUR SCORE

Total the number of "Mostly true" answers: _____

What it means:

0–3   Your library is still living in the last century. If your users are too, that's OK.

4–7   Good. Your library is waking up to the realities of the present. Take this quiz again every three months until your score improves.

8–11   Excellent! You have an open mind and a flexible attitude about change. Your library is learning to deal with ambiguity, the staple in a fast-changing world. Tackle the challenges you can deal with on your own; join with others to change what you can't do alone.

12   Congratulations! Yours is truly the twenty-first-century library, grappling with the important issues of the day. As you clarify each uncertainty, the changes you make to your work and services, including a virtual reference service, will be stronger, and you'll be rewarded with a supercompetent staff and a grateful and burgeoning clientele.

Think Like Your Clients Think

You're not so different from your demanding clients

When you are off duty, I'll wager you have the mind-set of your clientele. Namely, as a customer, you patronize services that have most, if not all, of the following ten characteristics:

- personalized
- convenient
- uncomplicated to use
- timely
- accurate
- accessible when you need them
- priced fairly and affordably, preferably free
- labor-saving, time-saving
- staffed with personable experts
- trustworthy

Library clients are no different. Therefore, one measure of your readiness for virtual reference is your willingness to appreciate your clients' discontent with library service when it does not measure up to one or more of these ten values, just as you, as a cus-

A. Old Thinking to Discard

How do we bring the remote users into the library?

Our goal is user independence. We expect users to find what they need themselves. When they don't know, we teach them how.

We'll wait till they come to us with a question.

We can expect clients who are in the library to come to the reference desk with their questions.

We serve up information on our terms, and when we ask our clients about their opinions, we customarily set the boundaries within our existing practices. We limit their responses by the choices we allow.

B. New Thinking to Adopt

How can the library become less remote from the users?

One size doesn't fit all. Different clients have different needs, and some clients have different needs at different times. So our goal should be to provide a variety of services that meet those different needs. Some will want (or require) instruction to know how to be independent users; some will want us to supply the answer ASAP. Both extremes, and variations in between, are justifiable needs. We need to become experts in our ability to judge the most appropriate service to give at the moment.

We'll go to wherever they are, situated where they can't ignore our presence. We'll be such an integral part of our clients' environment that we'll often know what they need without their asking, and we'll supply it. (Lipow, 1999)

We know many clients in the library have questions but, for a variety of reasons, don't ask them at the reference desk. We will use technology to bring the reference desk to them.

Technology is enabling us to "learn the user" as opposed to requiring the user to learn the library. We must truly begin to understand the changing desires of our users as they relate to knowledge and information, and tailor our services to satisfy those desires.

A. More Old Thinking to Discard

Our answers come only from quality sources.

B. More New Thinking to Adopt

Now that we have access to so much more information than would fit on our shelves, there are times when we find information whose reliability we cannot vouch for. Under some circumstances it is appropriate for us to dispense such information, and at those times we will always append a cautionary word about its questionable nature. Examples of times we might want to give dubious information to the client are when no other information on the user's topic can be found or the user wants everything imaginable on the topic. (See sidebar "Deliver bad information?" on the next page.)

The client at the desk has priority over the one on the phone. After all, the in-library client who took the trouble to get there deserves our attention over someone who doesn't make the effort.

We'll strive to give equivalent service to walk-in clients and those who come remotely via phone or Internet. After all, the barriers to getting to us—limited service hours, traffic and parking problems, lines at the desk—are insurmountable for too many of our clients. Also, clients in the library have many more options for finding what they need than does the information seeker who can't come to the library.

Our clients' reference questions are best answered by the staff in my library. We know our clients, and since our collections were built to meet their needs, it is most likely that what they are looking for is in our library.

Our clients are best served by a network of professional reference librarians who together can provide service 24 hours a day. They have access to similar information resources as we do, including our Web site and catalog of holdings, and can be trusted to refer clients back to their home library when that is what is called for.

Deliver bad information?

Here are two situations about experiences using questionable information.

1. In a "rethinking reference" workshop I facilitated, one participant asked the group for advice about how she should have handled the following situation: "A patron asked for information on traveling to Cuba. I found laws, relevant discussions in Congress, articles about consequences, and more. Everything I gave him embellished on the legal prohibition against travel to Cuba. He left, and returned several days later to inform me of a 'terrific chat group for people traveling to Cuba that my friend told me about. So I'm going via Canada, but I could have also gone via Mexico.' I replied that the reason I didn't consider chat groups and other similar resources was that I couldn't vouch for their reliability. He made a face that conveyed, 'OK, lady, stick to your rules instead of being helpful.' What should I have done?" The group agreed with the patron: she should have given him unconfirmable information, being sure to explain its lack of authoritativeness.

2. On an electronic forum, this question was posted under the heading "VR and news groups?": Any libraries with experience . . . [getting] help from the [news]groups/[chat]rooms? To which one librarian answered: ". . . getting help or info from the people in the chatroom/forums, etc. . . . is the reason most people use forums . . . . They want instant info from the people closest to the source. That is why I use them. Problem is that it is hard to verify the info as good or bad. That usually takes another step." (Hoyt, 2002)

[Excerpted from exchange on the e-group LiveReference, 6 July 2002]

tomer, may think about abandoning a nonlibrary service that disappoints you for the same reason.

Take a new look at old ideas

Another measure of your readiness for moving reference into the virtual environment is your openness to rethinking some sacred tenets reference librarians have lived by for generations. Exercise 2–2 lists some of those long-held beliefs (column A), and for each, the new mind-set that is required (column B). Before reading on, take time now to do this exercise. It may make a difference in how you interpret the rest of this book.

Exercise 2–2. Challenge long-held beliefs

Instructions: See pages 30–31. Read an old-think in column A, then consider its new-think counterpart in column B. Continue in this manner until you have given thought to each old-think/new-think issue. Your objective is to move yourself entirely from A to B or have convincing reasons for holding on to A.

Invent New Vocabulary

While you are rethinking your organizational structure and job assignments (as suggested in "Six Approaches to Carving Out a Niche for the New Service," pages 9 to 15), play around with new names for your departments and job titles. According to Robert Kegan and Lisa Laskow Lahey (2001), a change in your language will change your perception of it. They discuss conversational forms of language that dictate particular behaviors. That concept can be extended to include what you name a work function or activity. For example, librarians who call themselves or their departments something new and unfamiliar claim it frees them to think of their work differently. Thus, "informatician" is used in Finnish libraries; "information therapists" is what ethnographer Bonnie Nardi thinks reference librarians should call themselves; changing "reference service" to "concierge service" is library space planning consultant Andrea Michaels's recommendation to her clients; the University of Arizona libraries calls its former Reference Department "The Information Commons" and its reference librarians "Connection Developers." (See also comments in Exercise 2–1 on pages 27 to 29 about the possible limiting consequences of calling yourself "librarian.")

Keep Up with Progress

With changes occurring so rapidly in society at large, you'll need to keep an open mind about how new developments will affect your library and your job. Also, your library's ability to revise past decisions—even relatively recent ones—and make appropriate changes in a timely manner can be helped or hindered by objective conditions in the library. At the end of Chapter One, we discussed the desirability of being a learning organization, as conceived by Peter Senge, for keeping up with the times. In the reference realm, one measure of a learning organization is a staff informed of new developments as soon as they happen and new quality Internet resources as soon as they appear. This section is devoted to ways staff can stay current with issues and developments in technology and library innovation, as well as with late-breaking Internet resources.

New Internet resources and current developments

To keep abreast of newly appearing and newly discovered Internet resources:

- Regularly visit the weekly Scout Report (http://scout.cs.wisc.edu/report/sr/current/) and Research Buzz (www.researchbuzz.com).
- Subscribe to LII New This Week (http://lii.org/search/file/mailinglist).
- Regularly visit the Weblog The Virtual Acquisition Shelf & News Desk (http://resourceshelf.blogspot.com) and subscribe to its weekly Highlights (http://resourceshelf.freepint.com/update).
- Read the reviews of Internet sites that appear in regular columns of professional library journals such as "Off the Shelf and Onto the Web" in *Reference & User Services Quarterly.*

Current literature

An efficient way to keep abreast of developments in information technology is to subscribe to *Current Cites*, edited by Roy Tennant. This free monthly service is a list of citations of the best current literature in both print and digital form, selected and annotated by a team of library staff and sent to subscribers via e-mail. To learn more about *Current Cites* and how to subscribe to it, go to http://sunsite.berkeley.edu/CurrentCites/.

Developments to track

Standards for the processing of digital reference service transactions

An indication that virtual reference service is not just a passing fad is the formation of a National Standards Organization (NISO) committee to develop standards that enable interoperable, networked digital reference services. In January 2002, NISO, which is accredited by the American National Standards Institute to develop and promote technical standards for use in information delivery services, announced that this committee will develop a transaction protocol for interchange of messages between digital reference domains. This will support processing and routing of questions and responses and packaging of other information to be exchanged. The committee is also charged with building a metadata element set to identify and describe key components of questions and answers as well as institutional and personal data. NISO defines digital reference as a service allowing library clientele to submit questions and receive answers via electronic means, including via real-time chat and asynchronous e-mail. For information about NISO's progress in developing these standards, go to www.niso.org.

Legal issues

The Digital Reference Law Group (DRLaw), an independent research group formed in mid-2002, is investigating the legal issues related to digital reference, covering reference by e-mail, Web forms, chat, instant messaging, video, and Voice over IP. Its goal is to "develop guidelines and best practices useful to libraries, librarians, and governing authorities" in the areas of privacy and confidentiality, copyright and intellectual property, agreements and contracts (licensing and consortia, for example), and mandates and laws of governing bodies. The principals of this group are independent consultant and librarian Linda Arret (drlaw.arret@verizon.net), attorney Mary Minow (drlaw@librarylaw.com), and Cicely Wilson, librarian at FindLaw. Until the Digital Reference Law Group develops a Web site of its own, you may keep up with the broad range of legal issues related to libraries at Mary Minow's excellent Web site http://librarylaw.com.

Measurement and evaluation

To keep up with findings in important ongoing research to investigate and develop standards for assessing the quality of digital reference service, visit the Web site of the Information Institute of Syracuse University at http://quartz.syr.edu/quality. The study is being conducted by the Information Use Management and Policy Institute at Florida State University under the direction of Dr. Charles R. McClure with the assistance of Dr. R. David Lankes and the Information Institute of Syracuse.

Also, watch for the published results of John V. Richardson's study of measurement and evaluation of virtual reference services. Dr. Richardson, professor in the Department of Information Studies at UCLA, conducted this study throughout most of 2002, while a Presidential Scholar at Library Systems & Services (LSSI) in Germantown, Maryland.

Eliminating work

Keep an eye out for the latest systems that would automate certain library functions, such as check-in/check-out systems, sorting systems, or client notification systems. As one *Wall Street Journal* columnist reports, "As more people depend on the Internet for reference information they once had to be on location to get, libraries are giving patrons more at-home access, round-the-clock service and easier ways to check out material." In particular, the article showcases the Cerritos Public Library (http://library.ci.cerritos.ca.us.) in suburban Los Angeles, which resembles "more a theme park than a community center," for the all-out use of the latest technology, not only for its patrons (200 computer workstations, 1,200 laptop ports, multimedia rooms) but for the staff as well (for example, hand-held computers for librarians). Some work is eliminated altogether: its circulation system "uses radio frequency to track books instead of bar codes or magnetic strips. . . . [The system] automatically checks in books as they fall through the drop-off bin. Eventually, this wireless technology could allow cardholders to borrow books by simply walking out the door." (Sports, 2002: B12)

Search engine trends

"We're about to see the greatest mutation of the 'search' paradigm ever," claims Stephen Abram, as he reviews trends in a variety of technological developments, including search engines that search the invisible Web, motion digital video in DVDs and music; Web architecture; hardware; wireless; learning environments (collaboratories); and more. Examples of search engines that are expected

---

Speech recognition search engine

Eventually, we will be able to search for words in an audio file, such as a radio broadcast, or for an image, as in a TV show. See SpeechBot for a not-yet-effective effort at searching for audio and video content: http://speechbot.research.compaq.com/

to make present-day Google pale by comparison are those whose results include a visual display of the relationship among the retrievals, such as WebBrain, iLor, and Kartoo (Abram, 2002: 18–27). Another search engine, Teoma, claims (on its Web site) to "provide better results because it goes beyond traditional page ranking methods to determine authority in addition to relevancy."

Voice and video technologies

When the transmission of voice over the Internet gets as good as it is over the telephone, Voice over IP (VoIP) can be expected to be preferred over chat. And when it becomes commonplace that you and the caller can see each other, virtual reference will have all the advantages of an in-library service, at which point traffic can be expected to soar. However, reliable transmission of voice and video via the Internet is slow in coming. Desirable as talking to and seeing each other are, at present very few virtual reference software providers offer these capabilities. Those that do require that the client's computer be equipped with special software or hardware. They hold out the promise, however, that "soon," for voice interaction, the client will need only an applet, to be downloaded at the first use of your service. Many research groups are devoted to improving voice and video transmission. From time to time, visit the Web site of Internet2 Voice over IP Working Group at www.internet2.edu/voip/.

From the group's Web site: "The Voice over IP (VoIP) Working Group is designed to promote VoIP deployment within the Internet2 community. Utilizing the capabilities of the Abilene Network the working group will coordinate projects that will increase the knowledge base, disseminate information and help to drive standards of VoIP. The VoIP working group will cooperate with other Internet2 working groups that impact the VoIP process. These working groups include the Digital Video Working Group, the Quality of Service Working Group, the Measurement Working Group and others. The Working Group will also work with Industry to represent the needs of the Research Community in the development of VoIP products and standards. The Working Group will disseminate information through white papers and best practices that will result from VoIP research projects."

One-stop shopping, knowledge bases, and expert systems

The less information seekers need to know about which database holds the answer to their questions, the better. Requiring the searcher to first choose the resource and then conduct the search increases the likelihood of disappointing results. As all-in-one software improves, ever better results will be delivered to the searcher from a variety of sources without the searcher having to know about those sources in advance. Examples of organizations and products that are addressing this issue are the CAIRNS (Cooperative Academic Information Retrieval Network for Scotland) Project (http://cairns.lib.strath.ac.uk/); Muse Global (www.museglobal.com); MetaLib (a product of Ex Libris) (www.exlibris.co.il/metalib/); and ebrarian (a product of ebrary) (http://corp.ebrary.com/libraries/ebrarian.jsp)

Two projects to watch that could have an impact on one-stop-shopping developments are the National Library of Medicine's Unified Medical Language project (http://umlsinfo.nlm.nih.gov and www.nlm.nih.gov/pubs/factsheets/umls.html) and Universal Biological Index and Organizer (uBio), the pilot taxonomic name server project at the Marine Biological Laboratory in Woods Hole, Massachusetts, which is intended to enable more reliable cross-database searching among diverse formats and variant vocabularies (www.ubio.org)

Watch, too, developments in robotic question-answering technologies, known variously as "knowledge robots" or "knowbots," "bots," "agents," "avatars," and "infobots." These personal mediators have been on the horizon for decades, with early experiments in university laboratories and more recent dabblings in the commercial sector, but they are still rather primitive. They promise a world in which machines will replace human interaction. In a science-fictionesque scenario, librarian Ron Heckart speculates how a robot would replace human interactive library reference service. He gives a detailed account of how Alex, a university student, guided by his personal electronic avatar, consults electronic intelligent agents that help him prepare a research paper. "Alex completes the paper and posts it to the class Web site without ever visiting the physical library or talking to a real staff member." (Heckart, 1998: 254) In 2002, LSSI, a virtual-reference software vendor, took the lead in experimenting with the usefulness of bots in the virtual reference environment, using Kiwilogic's bot software (representatives of both organizations held a live online session on May 16, 2002, enabling participants to talk to Deborah the Bot), so perhaps progress in this area will develop at a faster pace than in the past.

The goal is to use such systems as front ends to your virtual reference service. Having a smart search engine intervene and process the question through an expert system as well as in databases containing information selected by librarians for their quality will reduce the need for connecting to your live service. The commercial reference service Webhelp.com, which charges a small fee to use its live reference service, runs your question against its FAQ file before bringing the live agent online, and if you end your transaction at that point, without making contact with an agent, you are not charged the fee.

Open source software

Proprietary software that drives search engines leaves you unable to explain or control the relevancy ranking of retrievals or know why this set of results was retrieved vs. that. There is a growing movement for open source software whose aim is to enable libraries to take control of the functionality of their systems. For discussions on the importance of open source software to libraries and librarianship, see the following:

David Dorman's "Technically Speaking" column in *American Libraries* (October 2001, page 82), titled "The Secrets of Search Software."

Dan Marmion's editorial "The Open Source Movement and Libraries" in *Information Technologies and Libraries* (December 2001, page 171).

The March 2002 issue of *Information Technologies and Libraries*, a theme issue devoted to open source applications in libraries.

Distance education, virtual universities

From time to time check the Distance Education Clearinghouse (www.uwcx.cdu/disted/home.html), which stays current with developments in formal remote teaching and learning programs. (Note that library services comprise very few of their concerns. We need to change that situation!)

Keeping up

Here are several ways that you can stay current with technological developments, library innovations, and late-breaking news.

1. Join the following electronic discussion groups that deal with virtual reference service:

- **LiveReference**
  Go to: http://groups.yahoo.com/group/livereference.
  Click on "Join This Group!" (right side of page).
  On the next screen, choose "Click Here to Register for FREE!"
  Fill out the various screens of registration.
- **DIG_REF**
  www.vrd.org/Dig_Ref/dig_ref.shtml
  www.vrd.org/Dig_Ref/DIGREFPolicies.shtml
- **Web4Lib, which includes virtual reference**
  http://sunsite.berkeley.edu/Web4Lib/

2. Watch the progress of QuestionPoint (see www.loc.gov/rr/digiref), a global reference project sponsored by the Library of Congress in partnership with OCLC, whose members are libraries throughout the world both providing and receiving service across time zones. (Until April 2002, the project was called Collaborative Digital Reference Service.)

3. Check out some of the resources listed in Peggy Hadid's (Multnomah County Library) list, "Web-based Reference Services" (www.multnomah.lib.or.us/ lib/products/ digref/ resources.html), which she keeps up to date.

4. Regularly visit sites that track the growth of virtual reference services.

- **Digital Reference site**
  http://pages.prodigy.net/tabo1/digref.htm
  Maintained by Stephen Francoeur at Baruch College; gives comprehensive coverage of all aspects of remote digital reference service, including definitions of the various forms of digital reference, software that's available, links to the libraries offering service, and more.
- **University of Leicester's Library Chat**
  www.le.ac.uk/li/distance/eliteproject/elib/chat.html
  Click on "Library Chat."
- **Registry of Real-Time Digital Reference Services**
  www.public.iastate.edu/~CYBERSTACKS/LiveRef.htm
- Lists (as links) by type of library those that are providing real-time reference service and the software each is using, and includes a good bibliography of articles on real-time reference services; maintained by Gerry McKiernan at Iowa State University.
- Visit www.lis.uiuc.edu/~b-sloan/digiref.html, Bernie Sloan's comprehensive bibliography of sources dealing with online/electronic/digital reference services, that is, the provision of reference services involving collaboration between library user and librarian in a computer-based medium, whether e-mail, Web form, chat, or video.

In fact, watch for anything produced by Bernie Sloan. He is the de facto chronicler of breaking developments in virtual reference and aggregator of current practices.

References

Abram, Stephen. 2002. "Let's Talk About It: The Emerging Technology Future for Special Librarians." *Information Outlook* 6, no. 2 (February): 18–27.

Asimov, Isaac. 1979. *Isaac Asimov's Book of Facts.* New York: Wings Books.

Baum, L. Frank. 1920. *Glinda of Oz.* New York: Ballantine.

Campbell, Jerry. 1993. In Search of New Foundations for Reference. In *Rethinking Reference in Academic Libraries.* Berkeley: Library Solutions Press.

Brenda Dervin and Patricia Dewdney discuss one or another aspect of the information seeker in all their articles, so you can't go wrong reading whatever either one writes, but see especially:

Dervin, Brenda, and Patricia Dewdney. 1986. "Neutral Questioning: A New Approach to the Reference Interview." *RQ* 25 (Summer): 506–13.

Dorman, David. 2001. "The Secrets of Search Software." Technically Speaking column, *American Libraries* (October): 82.

Heckart, R. J. 1998. "Machine Help and Human Help in the Emerging Digital Library." *College and Research Libraries* 59, no. 3: 250–59.

Hoyt, Sharon. 2002. "VR in news groups?" In LiveReference [Online]. Available: livereference@yahoogroups.com [6 July 2002].

Kegan, Robert, and Lisa Laskow Lahey. 2001. *How the Way We Talk Can Change the Way We Work.* New York: Jossey-Bass.

Kotter, John P. 1990. "What Leaders Really Do." *Harvard Business Review* (May/June): 103–111.

Lipow, Anne G. 1999. "In-Your-Face Reference Service." *Library Journal* (August): 50.

Marmion, Dan. 2001. "The Open Source Movement and Libraries." *Information Technologies and Libraries* (December): 171.

Nardi, Bonnie. 1998. "Information Ecologies." Keynote address at the Library of Congress Institute's "Reference Service in a Digital Age" [presented 30 June 1998]. [Online]. Available: http://lcweb.loc.gov/rr/digiref/archive/nardi.html [28 August 2002].

Sports, Kelly K. 2002. "Libraries Focus More on Upgrading Technology." *Wall Street Journal* (January 10): B12.

Van House, Nancy. 1991. "Reference Service in the '90s." Presentation to the library staff of the University of California, Berkeley.

Wachter, R. M., and L. Goldman. 1996. "The Emerging Role of 'Hospitalists' in the American Health Care System." *New England Journal of Medicine* 335: 514–17.

Zaleznik, Abraham. 1989. "Real Work." *Harvard Business Review* (Jan/Feb): 57–64.

Chapter Three
Shop Wisely for Software

To start your virtual reference service, you need virtual reference software, which falls into a category of software variously called "customer service software" or "call center software" or "Web contact center software." Originally developed for e-commerce, enabling businesses to give immediate, personalized service to their customers, now several dozens of systems are available, some of which are tailoring their software to the library reference environment. As you investigate the options, refer to this chapter for recommendations on making wise choices, some key issues to bear in mind, and software features to look for.

New vendors are sprouting everywhere, and every time you check up on the "old" ones—from the standpoint of libraries, going back to 1999!—they've added features and changed their prices. So any list in a book such as this one would be wrong as soon as it was printed. However, the Statewide Virtual Reference Project out of the Washington State Library tries to keep current a chart of comparative vendor information that includes software features, contact information, and much more, including (when the vendor supplies it) price. Bearing in mind that the information you get may be outdated, this is a good place to start for getting the lay of the land. Go to

http://wlo.statelib.wa.gov/services/vrs/textdocs/Vendormatrix.htm.

Keep a Flexible Attitude

The software you choose will either help or hinder the success of your virtual reference service, so you'll want to think through ahead of time as much as is feasible to reduce surprises. Remember that whatever you choose will change as new versions of your vendor's software appear and as other vendors offer more of what you want. Therefore, know what results you want before you make a purchase, but once your service is under way, stay ready to change your mind and your vendor as new possibilities open up.

Solicit Others' Opinions

Listen to the advice of colleagues who have gone through the shopping experience. A good way to find them is to visit either of the following sites that try to keep up with the changing virtual reference scene:

- **Digital Reference, maintained by Stephen Francoeur at Baruch College**
  http://pages.prodigy.net/tabo1/digref.htm
- **Registry of Real-Time Digital Services, maintained by Gerry McKiernans at Iowa State University**
  www.public.iastate.edu/~CYBERSTACKS/LiveRef.htm

There you will find links to libraries that are currently offering a virtual reference service, the software they are using, links to the vendors, and lots more invaluable information.

Another way to get the advice of experienced colleagues is to ask your question(s) of either of the two electronic discussion forums that exist for this very topic: LiveReference and DIG_REF.

To join the LiveReference e-group:
1. Go to http://groups.yahoo.com/group/livereference.
2. Click on Join This Group! (right side of page).
3. On the next screen, choose Sign up now to enjoy Yahoo! Group!
4. Fill out the various screens of registration.

To subscribe to the DIG_REF listserv:
1. Send an e-mail message to: LISTSERV@LISTSERV.SYR.EDU.
2. In the first line of the message, type:
   SUBSCRIBE DIG_REF Firstname Lastname

Also, see Lisa Roberts's excellent Chat Reference Software Checklist (which inspired several entries in these lists) at www.uncg. edu/~lcrober2/chatsoftware/checklist.html.

Library-based Issues

Checklists 1–4 on pages 43 to 44 are intended to encourage your deliberations about the impact of a virtual reference service on your library depending on the choices you make.

Exercise 3–1. Checklists of library-based issues to think through

CHECKLIST 1: Be aware of why you want to provide a virtual reference service

Check all that apply:
- ❑ Increase in clients who don't come to the library but who use the library from afar (e.g., distance education students)
- ❑ Decline in traffic at the reference desk
- ❑ Decline in walk-in traffic in the library in general or to use specific services (e.g., interlibrary loan)
- ❑ Decline in circulation of nonfiction printed materials
- ❑ Change in clients' methods for finding information
- ❑ Part of a larger effort to provide services to remote users (e.g., you're already using technology for remote instruction; you've launched related services such as document delivery)
- ❑ To be available in the same environment as the commercial references services so that clients have convenient access to quality information, regardless of format
- ❑ Opportunity to join with other libraries that want to include us in a network to share the staffing of the service
- ❑ We like trying new things
- ❑ Everyone else is doing it, so we should too
  [If you checked this one only, think again!]
- ❑ Other _____

CHECKLIST 2: Staffing the virtual desk

Check all that you want to try to achieve:
- ❑ Start small, with staff who are enthusiastic about this service; test the service with a pilot group in your community
- ❑ Separate the physical and virtual services
- ❑ Provide maximum hours of service, consider sharing the virtual desk hours with staff from other libraries
- ❑ Rethink current physical desk staffing and hours. Some ideas:

  - **Centralize your decentralized service points; throughout the library, place hotline phones that connect to the physical reference desk or computer stations that connect to your virtual reference desk**

  - **Put a triage desk near the library entrance staffed by paraprofessionals well trained in question-handling techniques, including when to refer on**

Staffing models

For a good description of alternative models for staffing the virtual reference desk, see *Starting and Operating Live Virtual Reference Services*, by Marc Meola and Sam Stormant (Neal-Schuman Publishers, 2002, pages 79–89).

CHECKLIST 3: Costs and budgeting

Keep in mind that among the virtual reference vendors, there are various charging schemes. For example, some are free; some charge a flat monthly fee; some charge a setup fee, plus a monthly charge for each "operator" or "seat" you buy. The number of operators or seats you have equals the number of incoming queries your service can handle simultaneously. At least one vendor charges a one-time setup fee plus an annual site-license fee that covers unlimited use by unlimited numbers of simultaneous operators.

Check all that you want to remember:

- ❏ Don't wait till you can afford it, but do wait till you know the range of prices for the available choices before you work out how to pay for the service
- ❏ List alternative sources of funding (e.g., operating budget, subscriptions budget, Friends group, grants)
- ❏ Budget items in addition to the software
  - Staffing the virtual desk
  - Administration (scheduling, monitoring use, reviewing transaction logs, building FAQs from the transaction logs)
  - Equipment
  - Training
  - Reconfiguring space
  - Publicizing the service

CHECKLIST 4: Use of licensed databases

If you will be sharing virtual desk hours with other libraries, and therefore will be serving clients from other jurisdictions when it is your shift, be sure your licenses allow you to use these databases when serving nonprimary clientele. Many libraries are renegotiating their contracts to cover virtual reference conditions.

Check all that you want to investigate:

- ❏ What are the limits of your current license regarding serving distant users?
- ❏ Can there be a maximum number of nonprimary clientele who receive service off of your licensed database without penalty or extra charges?
- ❏ What options are there for negotiating a special contract enabling the use of a library's licensed database when answering questions of all users of a networked service, regardless of whether they are from your community?
- ❏ What options are there for all librarians on duty in your virtual reference network to access your licensed database to answer the question when they don't subscribe to that database?
- ❏ What records need to be kept regarding the users of a networked service for purposes of monitoring compliance with the license?

Software-based Functions and Features

As you examine various brands, have a self-designed worksheet handy in which are included as many of the features listed in the following checklists as you want to consider—both the positive and negative features. Use the form in Figure 3–1, which outlines the key elements you'll want to include, as a basis for designing a worksheet relevant to your needs. Mark any feature that is a "must have" so you can eliminate quickly those that don't have it. You then have a basis for comparing the brands.

The functions and features listed here are intentionally not related to specific software brands and vendors because such information would be soon out of date. You can keep up with new software, new releases of existing software, and new software capabilities and features by visiting the services listed in the section "Keep Up with Progress" on page 33.

Figure 3–1 Example of a worksheet for evaluating software and elements to include

A file of this form, which you may use to customize it to your preferences, is on the CD-ROM that accompanies this book.

VIRTUAL REFERENCE SOFTWARE EVALUATION WORKSHEET

Vendor:
Contact name:
Phone:
E-mail address:
Web address:
Postal address:
Cost (including vendor's charging algorithm):
*** must have

	Has feature? (Y or N)	Has limitation? (Y or N)	Comments
Feature 1			
Feature 2***			
[etc.]			
Question 1	Answer:		
Question 2	Answer:		
[etc.]			
Special strengths			
Special shortcomings			

Exercise 3–2. Checklists of software-based functions and features

Vendor support may be the area to pay the most attention to. As the various brands of software begin to look more alike, what will distinguish one from another is their customer service.

CHECKLIST 5: The technology

Check out all of these technology-related items to be sure you cover basic issues:

- ❏ Chat: Where does the software reside? Who owns the content?
- ❏ Instant Messaging (see Foley, 2002: 36–45).
- ❏ Audio-Voice (Voice over IP): Eliminates the need to type the conversation (a drawback for the client and for posttransaction analysis is that there is no transcript of the conversation).
- ❏ Video (client can see you): Provides client with some of the visual cues missing in the chat environment.
- ❏ Client needs special software in addition to easily downloaded applets.
- ❏ Client needs special hardware.
- ❏ Where does the software reside?
  - • If ASP (Application Service Provider)—that is, the software resides with the vendor—does the library own the content? The FAQs? The knowledge base? If the library changes vendors, will the content be returned to the library? In a form that is transferable? What happens if the vendor goes bankrupt?
  - • If the library houses the software, what staffing is needed for installation? For maintenance? How will staff be trained?

CHECKLIST 6: The relative cost

Choose one that most closely matches your preference:

- ❏ High   ❏ Medium   ❏ Low   ❏ Free

CHECKLIST 7: Ease of use

Choose all that you want your system to include:

- ❏ Staff screen layout and vocabulary are user friendly
- ❏ Client screen layout and vocabulary are intuitive (i.e., not dense with text, well-designed screens that lead the eye to the function client expects to use, etc.)
  Note: It's a good idea to test this attribute with naive users
- ❏ Software works well with all major browsers and browser versions, and on IBM and Mac platforms

CHECKLIST 8: Adaptability

Choose all that you hope your system can handle:

- ❏ Library can customize screens
- ❏ Library can change vocabulary
- ❏ Library can create files of its own scripted, frequently used messages and URLs, and can specify their arrangement

❏ Individual virtual reference staff can create their own files of scripted messages

CHECKLIST 9: Library controls

Choose all that you hope will come with your system:

❏ Library can turn off service when it is not staffed
- **Client may submit question via e-mail form supplied by vendor; better if library can tailor the system's form or use its own form**
- **The service can be turned off on each staff member's computer, and only when all are off, does the client receive a message such as "We're not available at the moment. Please submit your question via e-mail/this form."**

❏ Sign-on procedures allow authentication of client

❏ Staff can monitor visitors to particular Web pages on the library's site, and detecting that the visitor might want help, can initiate a floating icon that invites the visitor to chat

❏ Librarian can include a third party, e.g., another client or another staff member (the staff member might be a trainee or a specialist brought in to advise)

❏ Librarian can refer client to other staff

❏ System has good, easily accessible transaction logs

❏ Librarian can code transactions as "completed" or "not completed" (see also Checklist 12, fourth item)

❏ System can produce good management reports
- **What variables can be searched and analyzed? The following are examples of what some systems provide: transaction logs, queuing patterns, time of day of queries, choices of dates (range, last week/month/year).**

CHECKLIST 10: Ease of access

Choose all that you want to check out:

❏ In the library, an ever present (persistent) link to the virtual reference desk
- **on browsers on public access computers in the library**
- **on all the library's Web pages**

❏ Remote computers can have an ever present (persistent) link to the library's virtual reference desk
- **on their desktops**
- **on their browsers**

CHECKLIST 11: Traffic management

Check all that you hope will come with your system:

❏ System enables automatic searching of client's question in the knowledge base before connecting client to staff, thereby screening out questions that don't need to be answered live

❏ System has good queuing and routing algorithms (based on load-sharing agreements and/or matching question to staff expertise) for distributing calls appropriately in a networked environment

❏ Computer alerts staff when new remote client arrives:
- **Pop-up box appears on the staff screen**
- **Computer makes a sound (e.g., dings, beeps, or best, customizable). . .**
- **. . . and continues to ring or beep reminders at specified intervals until the call is answered (as do some microwave ovens)**
- **Computer calls a pager**

CHECKLIST 12: Helpful communications handled by software

Check all that you hope will come with your system:

❏ Client in a queue is periodically told how long to expect to wait, based on software calculation of number ahead in queue and average length of transaction (for example, "There are three calls ahead of you; the approximate wait is 20 minutes. If you can't wait, leave a message . . . .")

❏ While you are busy searching, the client is automatically sent periodic messages (for example, "I'm working on it") that change as the wait lengthens ("I'm still working on it . . . .") at intervals you choose and using your scripts

❏ Client automatically receives an e-mailed copy of transcript soon after session has ended

❏ If client disconnects before the transaction has ended, the transcript of the session isn't transmitted to the client until the staff person has logged off, enabling the staff person to add information to the transcript (for example, "Sorry we were disconnected; here is more information.")

❏ For transactions coded "not completed," the system e-mails the appropriate staff person a reminder to follow up

❏ Computer indicates on staff screen "Client is typing" to prevent simultaneous cross-messaging; or, better, computer sounds a ding when client has sent a message

❏ When staff member is unable to get a response from a client who hasn't logged off but may be absorbed in an independent search, the staff member can interrupt the client or signal the client to indicate when ready to resume dialogue (enabling staff member to attend to another caller)

CHECKLIST 13: Feedback and assessment features

Check all that you hope will come with your system:

❏ System can produce transaction logs and a variety of good management reports for analyzing content and quality of interactions, traffic, staffing needs, costs, and user satisfaction

❏ System can automatically send client an evaluation form, online or via e-mail, immediately on ending a transaction and/or at a specified interval of time after the transaction has ended; library can specify an algorithm governing who gets the form

❏ System can automatically send client a survey

CHECKLIST 14: Practical functions

Choose all that you want your system to include:

❏ Librarian can push pages and files (articles, documentation) to client from a variety of sources

❏ Client can browse independently; that is, while staff person is busy searching for an answer, client can search too, and neither sees what the other is doing. For example, a staff person might push a particular Web site to the client and instruct the client in how to search that site, then leave the client to search independently while trying to find an answer

❏ Librarian can co-browse with client (where you go, client goes)

❏ Librarian can show client static slide shows, PowerPoint presentations, and such

❏ Staff and client can share the same space on the browser (whiteboard) to work together, including typing messages directly onto the screen, bypassing chat—a nice feature when instructing client

❏ System can handle problem sites or databases, such as those that would disrupt your or the client's browser, freeze the system, or disconnect the client

❏ System accommodates clients with disabilities, for example, it works well with screen-reading software used by a visually impaired client

CHECKLIST 15: Privacy and confidentiality

Choose all that you want to be sure to check out:

❏ Library can ensure confidentiality of transaction to client

❏ Client who so wishes can choose to be anonymous

❏ Library can choose to keep or discard transactions tied to client's contact information

❏ Client can allow or disallow library to keep an archive of client's transactions

❏ Library administrator can set levels of access to transactions and information about client

Software features that facilitate analysis and evaluation

For an example of management and assessment information that virtual reference software can produce, see *The Chat Reference Experience at Carnegie Mellon University*, by Matt Marsteller and Paul Neuhaus http://www.contrib.andrew.cmu.edu/~ matthewm/ALA_2001_chat.html

Vendor Support

> ### Exercise 3–3. Checklists of vendor support
> ### CHECKLIST 16: Quality of vendor's customer service
>
> Choose all that you want to learn about from the vendor:
> - ❏ Vendor understands libraries, library terminology, library reference service
> - ❏ Vendor provides excellent training
> - ❏ Vendor provides thorough, clear documentation
> - ❏ Technical support is readily available
> - ❏ Vendor provides back-up staffing or supplementary (e.g., during wee hours) reference service
>
> ### CHECKLIST 17: Vendor's viability
>
> Choose all that you want to learn about from the vendor and the vendor's library customers:
> - ❏ Number of libraries currently using the software
> - ❏ Assessment of the software and services by vendor's current library customers
> - ❏ If vendor ceases to exist, how easy is it for you to move to another vendor?
> - ❏ Technical support is competent and readily available

References

Foley, Marianne. 2002. "Instant Messaging Reference in an Academic Library." *College & Research Libraries* (January): 36–45.

Meola, Marc, and Sam Stormant. 2002. *Starting and Operating Live Virtual Reference Services*. New York: Neal-Schuman.

Part 2
Moving to the Virtual Reference Desk

The next three chapters cover the practical steps to take that will ensure a competently delivered service. Chapter Four has exercises that give you practice in the basic skills for working in the chat milieu. Chapter Five asks you to think about the policies to put in place, not only so that staff on virtual desk duty are guided in providing a consistent level of service but also to have a positive response to clients who ask about why you do thus and so, as well as to have a baseline from which to change as you learn what would work better. Then, because your virtual reference software is such an integral part of your interaction with the client, in Chapter Six you will consider how to take advantage of whatever flexibility there is in the software to customize it.

Chapter Four
Transfer What You Know to What You Do

Preventing the Einstellung Effect

Whenever you undertake learning a new skill, chances are you will be afflicted by the Einstellung Effect, the common human tendency to stop wanting to learn more the moment you have achieved the best results thus far. For example, if you are not taking advantage of sophisticated features of your word-processing software you'd find useful but you don't know about them because you haven't yet read the manual, you are a victim of the Einstellung Effect. Similarly, most online public catalog users use only the most obvious basic functions, because, content that the catalog yields so much with so little effort, they don't invest the time to learn its advanced timesaving functions.

In the virtual environment, the Einstellung Effect is likely to kick in as soon as you learn the least you need to know to conduct a minimally productive reference transaction. This chapter is intended to help you overcome the Einstellung Effect by leading you through exercises that will help you develop more advanced skills and strategies, enabling you to provide quality service that equals—even goes beyond—what you can do at the in-library reference desk.

A list of skills is included in "Basic Chat Etiquette" on page 54, followed by exercises that give you introductory experience in performing each of the skills. Completing these exercises will bring you to what learning theorists call the third stage of learning: Conscious Competent. Reaching the fourth stage of learning, Unconscious Competent, will take practice, practice, practice. (See sidebar "The four stages of learning" on page 55.)

All of the exercises are also on the CD-ROM that accompanies this book; you may change them or add others, increase the size of the font, or in any other way edit the exercises to make them most useful to you.

Basic Chat Etiquette

As you go through each of the exercises, bear in mind a few rules of thumb that are important to follow in an environment that lacks visual and auditory cues.

1. Do not keep the client waiting too long before hearing from you, so:

   a. Chat in short sentences.
   b. Develop the habit of clicking on SEND after one or two sentences.
   c. If your reply is long, break it up into small chunks, ending all but the last chunk with ellipses (...) that indicate "more is coming."

2. Do not use chat abbreviations (such as BRB, LOL, BTW), popular as they may be. Too many callers will be puzzled by them.

3. Avoid using other informalities, such as phonetic spellings ("This database is ez to use") or typing in all lowercase ("i'll check the french spelling").

4. Express your emotions cautiously. A simple, unambiguous smiley can be important to use if it follows words that might be misinterpreted—for example, "Sorry we were disconnected. Sometimes I think there are gremlins in our system. :-)"—or when you want to diffuse a potentially awkward situation with your sense of humor—"You want me to do your homework for you? Well, if you agree to sign my name to it . . . . ;-)" You may also use a bracketed word that describes your feelings, as in "<blush> Thanks for the compliment!"

5. To emphasize a word or phrase you want the client *not to miss* or be able to scroll back and find easily, put asterisks (*) around it. NEVER use all capital letters in conversation :-). It may be misinterpreted as anger or as shouting for special emphasis, as if you thought the client was stupid.

6. Work the client's name into the conversation. It conveys the sense that you are paying attention to the person as well as to the question. This practice is especially important at the outset if your software doesn't automatically insert it in a scripted opener, as in "Welcome to our service, Alice. My name is Anne. I see your request and have a quick question to ask before I start to look for an answer . . . ." or "Greetings, John! Wait just

a moment, while I . . ." Call the client by name at other times, as in "Check out this site, Alice, and let me know if it's in the ballpark."

7. Never begin a question to the client with "Why," as in "Why do you want this information?" "Why" conveys the message "Justify yourself!"

8. Ask for the client's approval before you implement a change ("I'd like to refer this question to our specialist. Is that OK with you?"), or when the client is "busy" doing something while you search ("I've found something I think is what you are looking for. May I send it to you now?").

Skills You Need When You Can't See or Hear the Client

You need a variety of skills to successfully handle transactions when you lack visual or auditory cues that are present in the physical environment. Below is a checklist of the most important of these skills. Exercises that give you practice in each of these skills follow the checklist.

- ❏ Get comfortable in cyberspace
- ❏ Perform a simple transaction efficiently
- ❏ Let your fingers do the talking and listening
- ❏ Answer the question the client hopes you heard
- ❏ Search in quality resources
- ❏ Evaluate retrievals
- ❏ Teach while you chat
- ❏ Control the length of a transaction
- ❏ Practice fixing what can go wrong
- ❏ Save your work to use again
- ❏ Put it all together
- ❏ Become overwhelmed

Skill 1. Get comfortable in cyberspace

Exercises 4–1 and 4–2 assume you are using Netscape or Internet Explorer. Each brand, or different versions of the same brand, may have slightly different ways of achieving a function, not to mention the variations between PCs and Macs. The instructions ask you to find or perform the function, but they are neither browser- nor platform-specific. Exercises 4–3 and 4–4 may be performed on either browser.

The four stages of learning

Stage 1 Unconscious Incompetent
You don't even know there is something to be learned. For example, you are a competent reference librarian starting to work at a virtual reference desk but without special training, so you apply in the virtual environment the skills that work well in the physical environment.

Stage 2 Conscious Incompetent
You read or hear about new skills to acquire that would improve the service you give at the virtual reference desk.

Stage 3 Conscious Competent
You go to a hands-on workshop, or use a manual such as this book, and try out the skills. They feel a bit awkward and you are relatively slow in executing them, but you can see their benefits.

Stage 4 Unconscious Competent
You practice and practice the skills until they become second nature and you apply them without thinking.

To move from Stage 3 to Stage 4 is the hardest and takes the longest amount of time because of the *un*learning of long-practiced habits that is required of anyone who has worked under an old system and must now work in a new way. The trick is to take the time to practice the skills until they are fully integrated into your repertoire of reference tools.

Exercise 4–1. **Know your browser's basic features**

If you haven't yet systematically reviewed the basic features of your browser, do so now, starting with the primary tool bars at the top of the screen, as shown in Figure 4–1 for Netscape, Figure 4–2 for Internet Explorer.

Step 1. Point your cursor to the top horizontal bar of your browser:

Title Bar Provides the name of the Web page that appears in the main window

Step 2. In the next bar, click on File, the first of the main headings that stretch across the bar:

Menu Bar (File, Edit, View, etc.) Pull-down lists of commands that control browser functions

Step 3. In the pull-down menu under File, click on each subheading and familiarize yourself with its function.

Repeat steps 2 and 3 for each of the other main headings along the bar (Edit, View, etc.).

Step 4. Repeat the above process for the next horizontal bar:

Navigation Bar (Back, Forward, Reload, Home, Print, etc.): **Shortcuts** (clickable icons) for changing locations and screen views, stopping the move to a different location, printing, and more

Be familiar with the following basic parts of a browser:

- Location or Address Box. It shows the URL of the current Web page and it is where you type a URL to change to another Internet location. Know the difference between a single click and a double click in the box. Know how to retrieve a list of the most recently searched URLs that were entered in this box for ease of reentering a URL.
- Icon on top right of screen. This is animated while the connection is being established, motionless when the connection is complete.
- Scroll bars (horizontal and vertical). Know what their presence and size tell you about the Web page.

Know where the following functions are located and how to use them for efficient searching:

- Bookmarks or Favorites
- Browser's preprogrammed sites
- Personal tool bar of links to sites you visit frequently
- History of searches in current session
- Find-in-this-page command

Figure 4–1 Primary horizontal bars on a Netscape browser

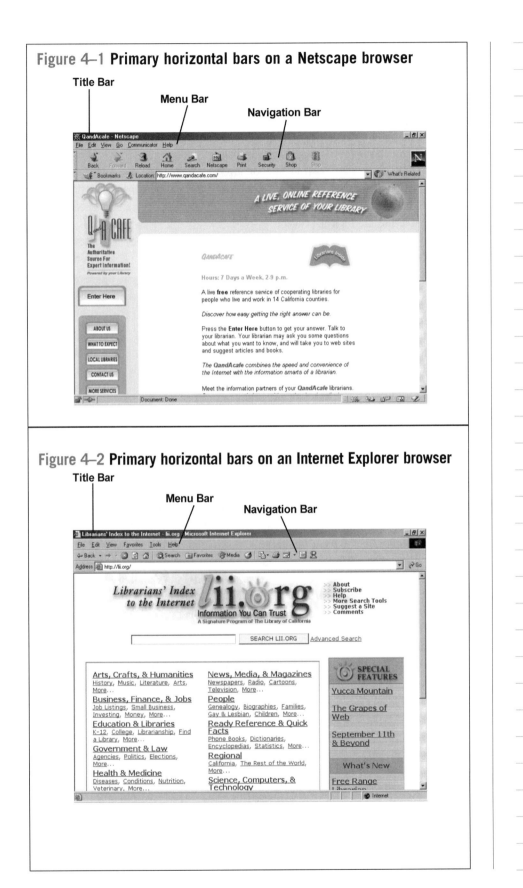

Figure 4–2 Primary horizontal bars on an Internet Explorer browser

Exercise 4–2. Be able to go beyond basics

Perform the following functions:

- Open three browser windows (File/New), go to different locations on each—for example, MetaCrawler (www.metacrawler.com), The Wayback Machine (www.archive.org), and the Scout Project (http://scout.cs.wisc.edu/)—and switch back and forth ("toggle") among them.

  Working simultaneously in different browsers enables you to manage the virtual reference desk efficiently. You can use one to conduct the transaction with the client, another one or two to search for answers, and perhaps another to respond to a second client.

- Use the FIND command to find a keyword or phrase of your choosing in a text-filled Web page; for example, at the Wayback Machine homepage, search for the word *Prelinger*.

  This is an efficient way to quickly find what you are looking for in a long Web page.

- Redo an earlier search out of sequence.
  Step 1. In Google (www.google.com), search for information about endangered species.
  Step 2. Go to two sites listed among the retrievals.
  Step 3. Repeat the search in Librarians' Index to the Internet (http://lii.org).
  Step 4. Go to two sites listed in this batch of retrievals.
  Step 5. Jump directly to the first Google retrieval by pointing to the BACK button and holding down the mouse button (in the newer Macs, the tiny button next to the BACK button, or click on GO on the Menu Bar), which produces a drop-down list of your previous searches. Highlight the result you want to retrieve. (Do not hit the BACK button repeatedly till the page appears.)

- Efficiently block a large section that spans more than one screen: Put your cursor at one end of the section. Hold down the SHIFT key, scroll to where you can see the other end of the section, and click at that point. The entire section should now be blocked. (You could now right-click on the blocked text to copy and paste, delete, etc.)

- Many browser functions can be achieved in more than one way. Learn those multiple ways, including those that use the context-sensitive menus that appear, for PCs, when you right-click the mouse, or, for Macs, when you hold down the mouse button for two or three seconds. In particular:
  a. Find three ways to go back to the previous screen—using Menu Bar, Tool Bar, and right-click (or holding down) of mouse button.
  b. Find two ways to jump over past searches to retrieve a previously displayed Web page.
  c. Right-click/hold down the mouse button in different locations on the screen and notice the functions that can be performed at that spot.
  d. Find three ways to copy and paste—using Menu Bar/Edit, CTRL or function key, and right-click/hold down the mouse button.

Exercise 4–3. **Know your software's bells and whistles**

Methodically experience every feature of your virtual reference software, learning its bells and whistles.

As you go through this exercise, assess how self-evident the client-side features are and how easy or difficult they are to use. Do the same for the librarian's side. To the extent they are not self-evident and you cannot change them for the better, these will be areas on which to focus the training of staff and ad hoc alerts to the client.

In particular, become very familiar with the following:

Client's side
- Procedure for accessing your virtual reference service
- Procedure for asking a question
- Procedure for chatting
- What happens when your service isn't open for business?
- What happens when things go wrong? (browser freezes, connection is accidentally broken)
- In what ways can the client make things go wrong? (uses own browser functions rather than those on the screen that your service generates)

Librarian's side
- Login procedures
- Logout procedures
- Options for connecting to waiting client
- How to create, organize, and use scripted messages
- Options for pushing and sharing pages (Send Page, Escort, Co-browse)
- Options for closing a session
- Post-transaction procedures
- Options for sending snapshots of special database pages, slide shows, and other materials not resident on the Internet or that require special software to view
- What happens when things go wrong? (browser freezes, connection is accidentally broken)
- In what ways can you (inadvertently, of course) make things go wrong? (use own browser functions rather than those on the screen that your service generates)

Exercise 4–4. Understand the information landscape on the Internet

If you haven't received formal training in using the Internet for ready reference, arrange for such training now. Knowing the types of print resources in your library's reference collection as well as the catalog structures for finding specific examples within each type enables you to choose the most likely source first; similarly, knowing the types of Internet resources and how to find specific resources within them will reduce transaction times and get the best results.

At minimum, here is what you should know:

a. When and how to access the "invisible Web" or "deep Web"
   Visit:
   www.invisible-web.net
   www.invisibleweb.com

Read:
Bergman, Michael K. 2001. "The Deep Web: Surfacing Hidden Value." *Journal of Electronic Publishing* 7, no. 1 (August) [Online]. Available: www.press.umich.edu/jep/07-01/bergman .html [28 August 2002].

b. Quality subject directories maintained by librarians and other experts
   Check out:
   Librarian's Index to the Internet (http://lii.org)
   Infomine (http://infomine.ucr.edu)
   Web Feet Online (available to paying subscribers only; details available at www.webfeetguides.com.)

c. Strengths and shortcomings of the various search engines
   Go to Infopeople's Search Tools Chart
   www.infopeople.org/search/chart.html
   and its Search Engines Quick Guide
   www.infopeople.org/src/guide.html

d. How to structure your query in search engines for the most relevant results

For example:

Step 1. In Google, enter the following search and notice the number and nature of retrievals:
"sperm whales" +research +rescue +.edu -dolphins -dolphin -sharks -humpback -blue

Step 2.. Delete the last keyword and its accompanying command (-blue), search and notice the number of retrievals.

Step 3. Repeat Step 2, eliminating the last keyword each time, searching and noticing the number of retrievals, until you are down to "sperm whales."

Step 4. Delete the quotation marks around *sperm whales*, search and notice the number of retrievals.

To gain a sense of the range and complexity of the skills and knowledge you need for providing service in the digital environment, check out the titles and descriptions of classes for California public librarians by visiting the Infopeople Project at www.infopeople.org and clicking on Training.

Skill 2. Perform a simple transaction efficiently

Practicing exercise 4–5 will enable you to become comfortable with the basics of a virtual reference transaction.

Exercise 4–5. Greet the client, conduct a simple dialogue, push a page, and end the transaction

You and a colleague take turns being the librarian and client.

Step 1. Client logs on and asks the following question:
What is the state bird of Hawaii?
Step 2. Librarian greets the client with a scripted message and answers the question by pushing the following Web page to the client:
www.50states.com/bird/nene.htm
Step 3. Librarian asks client whether this answers the question.
Step 4. Client answers *Yes, thanks* and ends the transaction.
Step 5. Librarian ends the transaction according to software procedure and library policy.

Repeat until you are comfortable with these basic procedures: log on with a greeting, chat, use a scripted message, push a page, and close the transaction.

Skill 3. Let your fingers do the talking and listening

Exercises 4–6 through 4–9 give you practice in compensating for the lack of visual and auditory cues in the chat environment. For some specific ways to accomplish this, see Appendix 4, Chat Communication Tips (pages 173 to 175).

Exercise 4–6. Feel the effect of silence

When you and the client can't see or hear each other, you need to compensate for the lack of visual cues that give each of you valuable information. A rule of thumb is to communicate something to the client at least every 30 to 45 seconds. A minute of waiting in silence can seem an eternity.

Try this:
Test yourself with a colleague in a telephone conversation. Tell the colleague you'll be right back, then count out 60 seconds in silence so you both can experience the mounting sense of uncertainty about whether you are still connected.

Exercise 4–7. Fill the client's dead time

If your software doesn't regularly and automatically let the client know what you are doing after about 30 seconds of no activity (with a message such as "The librarian is typing you a message" or "I'm working on your question" and, after specified intervals, "I'm still looking. Thanks for your patience" or "I'm almost there"), you will need to let the client know what you are doing and when to expect to hear from you. Conversely, if your software doesn't let you know what the client is doing (for example, "Client is typing a message to you" or "Client is searching in browser"), you will need to ask the client questions to be sure he or she is still there.

For this exercise, you and a colleague take turns being the librarian and client.

Step 1. Client asks one of the following questions (each client should ask a different question) or another of your choosing:

What are the ideological and religious differences between Christians, Jews, Buddhists, Hindus, and Muslims?

I want whatever there is on pop-up books, including their history and how to make them.

Step 2. Librarian searches the Internet and the library's licensed databases, and checks the library's online catalog for print resources. Every 45 seconds, send a message that assures the client you are still working on the question. End each message with a yes-no question ("Is that OK with you?"; "Are you finding anything useful in the resource I gave you to search?") to encourage the client to send a response, letting you know he or she is still with you.

Exercise 4–8. Avoid embedding negative emotions in your message

Be aware of the subtle ways you may be expressing negative emotions, unwittingly making an accusation, or trying to convey "It's not my fault." With a colleague, review each of the messages below as follows:

Step 1. Imagine a client's negative reaction to the librarian's well-intentioned messages.

What emotion(s) might the client "hear" in your words?

Step 2. Think about what the librarian had hoped to convey by the message.

Step 3. Rewrite the message in an unambiguously positive way.

Delivering bad news

I'm sorry but the best answer is in a database that I am not authorized to use with our nonprimary clientele such as yourself. Here's something else that might do.

- Client's reaction?
- What had you intended to convey?
- Your rewrite: _____

Emphasizing a point

If you had read our homepage, you'd know we do NOT answer questions about _____ [crossword puzzle contests/genealogy/legal or medical advice—you fill in the blank].

- Client's reaction?
- What had you intended to convey?
- Your rewrite: _____

Requesting clarification

Please rephrase your question more clearly.

- Client's reaction?
- What had you intended to convey?
- Your rewrite: _____

Reacting to a situation you haven't dealt with before

Hmmm . . . Most people don't have the trouble you're having using this resource. . . .

- Client's reaction?
- What had you intended to convey?
- Your rewrite: _____

Personal asides

Let me know whether this site interests you. It advocates a weird viewpoint, but it's by a reputable author and deals directly with your question.

- Client's reaction?
- What had you intended to convey?
- Your rewrite: _____

> ### Exercise 4–9. Control your negative reaction to the client's message
>
> Responding to the client's messages below, turn your negative reaction to a positive return message according to these guidelines:
>
> - Suppress the urge to "get even" or to show who is really in control. (Bad: "I've spent as much time on your question as I'm allowed. You should come to the library for more extended help.")
> - Don't respond defensively. (Bad: "I'm doing the best I can.")
> - Respond with a friendly smile in your words. (Good: "I was really off track!")
> - Avoid "I'm sorry, but . . . ." "But" undoes "I'm sorry," and "I'm sorry" highlights how *you* feel (about which the client couldn't care less), when you should be showing concern about how the client feels.
>
> Client: *Can you please hurry up? I don't have much more time to spend on this.*
> Your negative reaction: _____
> Your positive response: _____
>
> Client: *What you sent me has nothing to do with what I asked for. Can you do better?*
> Your negative reaction: _____
> Your positive response: _____
>
> Client: *I don't think you understand my question. It might be better if you refer me to someone who might be more helpful.*
> Your negative reaction: _____
> Your positive response: _____

Skill 4. Answer the question the client hopes you heard

This section provides practice in using the reference interview technique known as neutral questioning (NQ) as a first response to the virtual reference client's question. For a description of the concepts underlying the technique, its characteristics, its special application in the virtual environment, and examples of neutral questions, see Appendix 2 (pages 157 to 160).

At the physical reference desk, as a rule, you follow the client's question with a two- or three-question interview that starts with a "neutral question" to ensure you'll be working on answering "the real question." If pressed for time, you may shorten how long you spend on finding an answer ("Your question will take longer than we have time for right now, so let me start you off with this resource. Come back when you're ready for more . . . ."), but you usually don't skimp on that initial brief interview because it will result in a more efficient use of time in the long run.

In the chat medium, however, in which the question comes to you in text form, the client's words may seem less tentative, more thought out ("If it's in print, believe it"), so you are likely to start your fingers flying over the keyboard as soon as you see the question. Because skipping that initial interview can lead to wasting precious time, you'll be a more efficient searcher if your knee-jerk response is a neutral question rather than simply jumping immediately to answer the question as first asked.

For exercises 4–10 through 4–15, you and a colleague take turns being the client and librarian. Using your virtual reference software, conduct the online reference transactions as described. In all cases, the client's question is not "the real question."

In exercises 4–10, below, and 4–11, on page 66, follow the scripts as given. They will help you understand the benefits of routinely opening with a neutral question.

The additional exercises (4–12 through 4–15) will help you develop a sense of which variation of NQ is appropriate to use in response to different types of questions.

Exercise 4–10. Omit the neutral question

Client: *I am looking for a copy of the Van Gogh painting called* Girl with Ruffled Hair.

Librarian: Greet the client and add:
The Van Gogh Gallery is a good place to start. Just a moment and I'll see what I can find.
Go to www.vangoghgallery.com.
Click on Paintings/Thumbnail Version.
Then, in the Alphabetical Listings, scroll down and click on G,
then on Girl with Ruffled Hair ("The Mudlark").
Send that page to the client's browser, and ask *Is this the painting you were looking for?*

Client: *Yes, that's it. Thanks so much!*

Both client and librarian end the transaction.

Exercises to practice neutral questioning, virtual-reference style

Instructions for Exercise 4–12 on pages 67–68

To do the exercise properly, you will need to review Appendix 2 (pages 157 to 160), especially the section Modify the Technique for the Virtual Environment, which calls for providing the client with a quick, tentative answer and simultaneously asking a neutral question that starts with an opener. For example:

Opener. *If I understand your question, here is a document that provides some information. I can vary the search in several ways, depending on your situation. . . .*
. . . followed by a neutral question, such as
Can you say more about what you are hoping to find?

Step 1. Client asks the question as specified.

Step 2. Librarian responds with a quickly retrieved Internet resource sent to the client's browser and simultaneously asks a neutral question.

Step 3. Client comments on the resource displayed and then, after reading the "situation," answers the neutral question in his or her own words.

Step 4. Librarian, now knowing the "real question," continues the transaction accordingly.

Exercise 4–11. **Use NQ to get at the real question**

Client: *I am looking for a copy of the Van Gogh painting called* Girl with Ruffled Hair.

Librarian: Greet client and add: *There are a few ways to search for this, depending on what specifically you are looking for. Can you describe what you are hoping to find?*

Client: *I'm a painter and I want to paint this Van Gogh as a present for my daughter, who looks just like the girl in the painting, messy hair and all! I want to make the painting in the original dimensions, but the copy I have shows the dimensions in centimeters. I was hoping the copy you found for me would give the dimensions in inches.*

Librarian: *Oh, so if you give me the dimensions in centimeters and I get them converted to inches, will that fill the bill? Or will you still need the copy of the painting?*

Client: *Oh no, I don't need the painting itself, just the dimensions in a form I can understand. My copy gives the measurements as 35.5 cm. x 24.5 cm.*

Librarian: Now that you know the real question, look for a site that converts centimeters to inches.

End the transaction and discuss the difference between Exercises 4–10 and 4–11.

Skill 5. Search in quality resources

Exercise 4–13 on page 69 gives you practice turning first to a quality resource, including one in print, rather than to a common search engine such as Google. Use what you learned about the "deep Web" (Exercise 4–4, page 60) and what you know of your library's electronic and print resources to answer the questions.

Exercise 4–12. Asking neutral questions that start with openers

US cities

Client: *Can you show me an atlas with topographical maps of US cities?*

Librarian: Send a specific resource followed by NQ.

Client: Respond as in Step 3 on page 66.

Situation: Your doctor told you that you have to move to a climate with low carbon monoxide concentrations if you want to live longer than a year, so you are looking for cities that have low carbon monoxide levels. You've been told that cities more than 3,000 feet above sea level meet that criterion, so you're checking out which cities are above that altitude.

Librarian: Proceed to answer the real question.

Vietnam War

Client: *I'm looking for a comprehensive book on the Vietnam War.*

Librarian: Send a specific resource followed by NQ.

Client: Respond as in Step 3 on page 66.

Situation: Your uncle, a Vietnam veteran, has been having nightmares recently and you think they are related to his war experiences, which included killing enemy soldiers and destroying entire villages. You are hoping that a book covering the Vietnam War in depth will contain information about the psychological effects of such experiences.

Librarian: Proceed to answer the real question.

History book

Client: *I'm looking for a book by Myers or Meyer or something like that. I don't recall the title, but it's on American history during the revolutionary period.*

Librarian: Send a specific resource followed by NQ.

Client: Respond as in Step 3 on page 66.

Situation: You saw a review of recent books on the revolutionary period of American history, and this one included information about the signers of the Declaration of Independence. You think you are a descendent of Button Gwinnett, one of the signers. You want to find out more about Gwinnett and thought you'd start with this book.

Librarian: Proceed to answer the real question.

> ### Building fences
>
> | | |
> |---|---|
> | **Client:** | *Can you help me find a book or article about building fences between two residential properties?* |
> | **Librarian:** | Send a specific resource followed by NQ. |
> | **Client:** | Respond as in Step 3 on page 66. |
> | **Situation:** | You are having trouble with your neighbor. You've recently built a fence along your property line that borders on your neighbor's, and your neighbor is furious and making your life miserable. You want to find a way to get along with your neighbor and hope that a book or article about fence building will offer guidance in that area. |
> | **Librarian:** | Proceed to answer the real question. |

Skill 6. Evaluate retrievals

When you recommend to your client a print resource chosen by your library, you need not worry about its quality because it has been preselected by a librarian who has filtered out the junk. In the virtual environment, however, unless you search in a preevaluated resource such as the Librarians' Index to the Internet (http://lii.org), you must assess the quality of an unfamiliar retrieval before you turn it over to your client. Exercise 4–14 on page 69 gives you guidance in how to evaluate Web sites, and Exercise 4–15 on page 70 gives you practice putting to use what you learned in Exercise 4–14.

Skill 7. Teach while you chat

In some ways, the virtual reference desk can be a better medium than the physical desk for providing instruction. For example, if your software allows the client to accompany you as you conduct a search, or enables you to transfer the cursor to the client and watch while the client follows your instructions for searching in a particular resource, and then sends to the client an e-mail containing the transcript of the entire transaction, the likelihood that what you taught will be revisited and retained is greater than if you transmitted the same information to the client over the physical counter. Exercises 4–16 and 4–17 on page 70 will give you practice in integrating instruction into your virtual ready-reference session.

Exercise 4–13. **Avoid Google, remember print**

Working in pairs, alternate roles as librarian and client. For each question asked by the client, the librarian should do the following:

a. Assume the question is the "real" one (that is, think—but don't ask—a neutral question).
b. If your software allows, put Google on the client's browser and tell the client to search there while you search elsewhere.
c. Search for an answer in Web-based quality subject directories, and name one print resource you will check later.

Client's questions

1. *I'm looking for a legislative history of the California lottery. I'll be participating in a debate in two days.*
2. *I'm planning a lesson for my freshman college students in building model bridges. I need blueprints or designs for different types of bridges. Can you help me?*
3. *Where can I write to J. K. Rowling to tell her how thrilled I am with her books?*
4. *I'm trying to find the closing price for General Electric stock on November 20, 1999.*

Exercise 4–14. **Know how to evaluate retrievals**

Step 1. Go to the Evaluating Web Pages Web site, designed by Joe Barker: www.lib.berkeley.edu/TeachingLib/Guides/Internet/Evaluate.html.
Step 2. Read the entire page.
Step 3. Evaluate each of the sites linked under "Try assessing the authenticity and integrity of these groups of web sites." (Click on Hints and Tips as needed.)

Skill 8. Control the length of a transaction

When you need to limit the time you spend with a client at the physical reference desk (for example, it's nearly closing time, or others are waiting in line), you have a keen sense of timing and know how to pace yourself and the dialogue accordingly to provide in the time allotted a part of the answer as well as a recommendation for how to get more information. You will want to do the same at the virtual reference desk, but there the alerts for when to impose such limits are different, so you will need to use new clues to become aware of your virtual surroundings and of the passing of time. Exercises 4–18 and 4–19 on pages 71 and 72, respectively, will get you started in developing these perceptions.

Exercise 4–15. Practice evaluating retrievals

Working in pairs, alternate roles as librarian and client for the questions below. For each question asked by the client, the librarian should do the following:

a. Assume the question is the "real" one (that is, think—but don't ask—a neutral question).
b. Search for an answer.
c. Before you show the client what you found, evaluate the quality of the retrieval and convey your assessment to the client.
d. After completing a transaction, conduct a brief postmortem.

Client's questions

1. *How many "close encounters" are there? I know about "Close Encounters of the Third Kind." Are there other kinds? If so, what are they? Who invented them?*
2. *Can you tell me when daylight saving time was introduced in the US?*
3. *What are the criteria for the Malcolm Baldrige National Quality Award for education?*
4. *What alternative cures for macular degeneration are being tried? How can I find out who is doing cutting-edge research in this area?*

Exercise 4–16. Tell the client what to do next time

Repeat questions 1 and 2 in Exercise 4–15. Practice this exercise with a colleague, taking turns being the client and the librarian.

Librarian: Find a resource that answers the question. Before you conclude each session, begin a sentence to the client as follows:

The next time you have a question like this, here's how to go about finding an answer: _____ [complete the sentence in your own words].

Exercise 4–17. Observe each other conducting a search

If your software allows the client to observe as you search the Web, repeat one of the questions in Exercise 4–15. With the client looking over your virtual shoulder, explain what you are doing and why you chose to do it, point out what you want the client to notice, and show how you evaluated a retrieval.

If your software allows the client to search independently while you observe (and you have pretested your software's ability to handle the type of site you plan to turn over to the client's control), instead of performing the search yourself, watch while the client follows your step-by-step instructions, and point out what you want the client to notice.

Skill 9. Practice fixing what can go wrong

Just as it is important that you occasionally go through the steps of a fire drill in your library, so too should you be prepared for emergency situations in the virtual environment.

Your aim is to reduce unwelcome surprises, both for you and for the client. To this end, whenever you notice a glitch in your service, either remove the cause or change the clients' expectations by alerting them to the conditions that trigger the problem and providing advice about how to deal with it. Exercises 4–20 and 4–21 on page 73 will give you practice in trouble-shooting technical problems.

Exercise 4–18. Describe your virtual surroundings

As you help someone at the in-library desk, by quick glances at your surroundings you are aware of people waiting in line, other staff at the desk, what the client is doing at the moment (listening, talking, reading something you have supplied), the client's mood (happy, worried, impatient), or what the client is expecting to happen next (because of what you know the client can see and hear). At the cyberdesk, you need that information, but you get it by reading or typing.

For practice in heightening your awareness of the virtual environment, duplicate the following scene with three colleagues: Each of you should take turns being the librarian on duty, Client 1, and Client 2 or 3.

Step 1. Client 1 logs in and asks a question (for example, *Next week I will travel to _____ to learn about _____* [Denmark/Hans Christian Andersen; Australia/aboriginal cave paintings; Arizona/Frank Lloyd Wright]. *Where specifically should I visit?*

Step 2. Librarian greets the client; while conducting a dialogue, and searching, and pushing pages that might answer the question . . .

Step 3. Clients 2 and 3 log in with questions (for example, *What has been written in response to Nicholson Baker's concern that libraries have abandoned their responsibility for preserving newspapers?* and *What are the e-mail addresses of all 100 US senators?*)

Step 4. Librarian: STOP what you are doing and take stock of what you know about the three clients:

- What is Client 1 doing? Thinking? Expecting to happen next?
- How long has Client 1 been waiting for a response from you?
- How long had the other two been waiting before you noticed them?
- How long had the other two been waiting before they received a response?
- What do the other two know about how long their wait will be?
- What do the other two know about alternatives to pursue if they do not want to wait?

Repeat this exercise until you know the answers to these questions without having to ask them.

Exercise 4–19. Limit your transactions to ten minutes

With a timer (either a mechanical one or a person), repeat exercise 4–12, except this time, end each transaction ten minutes after starting it, even if you have not completely answered the question.

After concluding each transaction, review the results to be sure they include the following:

- The start of an answer (relevant material, or referral to resources the client can examine later)
- A promise that you or a colleague will follow up the next day
- The routine for ending an incomplete transaction (that is, coding the transaction appropriately using the method provided by your software, and the procedure for sending you or the colleague a reminder the next day)

Skill 10. Save your work to use again

One of the most beneficial aspects of virtual reference service is the ability to capture and save your work and that of your colleagues. In a face-to-face transaction, you put effort into understanding the question and then draw on your vast store of specialized knowledge to solve the client's problem, and when the transaction is done . . . poof! All your work evaporates into thin air. No one, including you, can take advantage of your work to deal with similar questions later, nor can you derive benefits from others' good work. In addition, your work cannot be used in training others, and the work of trainees on the desk cannot be reviewed to enable a trainer to see the gaps in knowledge or behavior that need attention. Exercise 4–22 on page 74 is intended to make you aware of the post-transaction features of your software that can be used to everyone's benefit.

Skill 11. Put it all together

Now that you have practiced each skill individually, try performing an ever-increasing number of activities simultaneously.

Exercise 4–20. Recover from a client-initiated disconnect

In pairs, take turns being the client and the librarian.

Step 1. Client asks a question: *Where should I look to learn how to read hieroglyphics?*

Step 2. Librarian finds a relevant resource to send to the client's browser.

Step 3. Client "accidentally" disconnects (by hitting a disconnect button, or in other ways your software can make that happen).

Step 4. Librarian notices what happens on the librarian's side and tries to reestablish the connection (via phone call, e-mail, or whatever other ways you can think of).

Step 5. Consider how you would prevent that type of disconnect in the future.

Exercise 4–21. Practice recovering from other surprise interruptions

Step 1. Keep track of what goes wrong during an interactive transaction (for example, your software doesn't allow you to transfer to the client's side material from proprietary electronic databases or Web pages containing frames, causing the browser to freeze or to take over the entire screen; important information is situated in an inconspicuous place on the screen or is ambiguously worded, and thus is missed or misinterpreted).

Step 2. Conduct virtual reference service drills in which you cause something to go wrong in the midst of a transaction, and then go through a recovery procedure. (When you are satisfied with a particular recovery procedure, be sure to train other staff in that procedure.)

Step 3. Repeat this drill for each of the problems you have encountered.

Step 4. For those problems caused by the software, work with your vendor to revise the software to eliminate the problem. To correct problems caused by human error, make the necessary changes, such as redesigning the screen, rewording the instruction, or renaming the button. When the problem can't be fixed, be sure to let the client know the circumstances that trigger the problem.

Exercise 4–22. **Perform post-transaction duties**

Make a list of the activities your software enables for examining and analyzing the transactions. For example:

- View transcripts of past transactions, grouped in categories you designate.
- Produce statistical reports about clients, completed and incompleted transactions, referrals, and so on.
- Edit transcripts as appropriate for inclusion in a staff-only or publicly available FAQ file.

Then, with a colleague, repeat questions 3 and 4 in Exercise 4–15.

After concluding the transaction, perform whatever post-transaction procedure is required for accomplishing each of the activities in your list.

Exercise 4–23. **Perform multiple tasks simultaneously**

Take turns being client and librarian.

Step 1. Client asks one of the following questions:

- *Can you recommend three or four books about poverty in the US? My 12–year-old daughter needs them for a book report. The report should be 800 words, so general information with some statistics would be ideal.*
- *I bought* The American Boy's Book of Sports and Games *at a garage sale. It was published in 1864 by Dick and Fitzgerald. I'm hoping I found a treasure. Can you tell me how much it is worth?*

Step 2. Librarian conducts the transaction using as many of the skills learned in the previous exercises throughout the session, including some performed simultaneously:

- Use software deftly: greeting, using scripted messages, closing.
- Use neutral questions (to which the client ad-libs a response).
- Search for answer in preevaluated resources.
- Check in regularly with client.
- Assess client's mood of the moment.
- Evaluate retrievals.
- Provide instruction relevant to the client's question.
- Perform post-transaction duties as appropriate.

Skill 12. Become overwhelmed

You are now ready to test your skills under pressure. In Exercise 4–24 you will practice being deluged with more traffic than you can handle. Then, when you are ready to go public, offer the service to a targeted subgroup of your entire community. Make them aware of their special responsibility in submitting questions and evaluating the responses to help you work the bugs out of your new service.

Exercise 4–24. Become overwhelmed

Ask far-flung colleagues to test your service.

Step 1. Choose two–hour blocks of time on particular dates when the full number of "agents" allowed by your contract can be on deck to give simultaneous service to callers.

Step 2. Decide on the maximum length of time you will spend with each caller in this experiment.

Step 3. About one week before the chosen dates, go to two or three heavily trafficked electronic discussion forums (such as LiveReference, DIG_REF, Libref-L, Web4Lib), and ask for help in testing your service. Invite participants to ask a question and tell them what to expect:

- Mention the amount of time you will spend with them.
- Explain that if you don't answer their question in the specified length of time, you will indicate how you will follow up, but in fact they are not to expect you to follow up.
- Ask them to evaluate their experience.
- Tell them that a benefit to them of their participation is the experience of using a chat service as a client and the chance to learn some specifics from you about your service (software, staffing, etc.), information that you will include in a brief description of your service that you will send to each volunteer.

Chapter Five
Update Your Library's Policies

This chapter provides guidance in developing policies and implementation guidelines related specifically to a virtual reference service. As you consider each of the topics, you will need to decide to what extent, if any, your virtual reference policy would affect other policies. If you are a single library system providing virtual reference service, you will probably need to amend your current policies and train staff on the new practices consistent with those policies. If you are a network of library systems cooperating to provide service, you will need to come to an agreement about these policies and corresponding practices, a process that may require some libraries in the network to change some of their longstanding local policies and practices. The policies cover the following issues:

- eligibility
- confidentiality
- use of licensed databases to answer questions
- how you will identify yourself to the client
- delivery of material to the client
- average length of transaction
- client satisfaction
- inappropriate client behavior
- questionable questions
- limit of transactions per client
- follow-up

(*Note:* The exercises for drafting policies on these topics, as well as the questions posed, are also on the CD-ROM that accompanies this book for easy editing.)

After you have drafted a policy, jot down ideas for implementing it. The implementation of a policy ensures consistency in training staff, which will result in a service of uniform quality. Once you settle on a policy and guidelines for its implementation, decide where among your virtual reference service Web pages and elsewhere your explanation of the policy to potential service users will go.

For ideas that will help you work out your policies, review the sample policies of other libraries in Appendix 3 (pages 161 to 171).

Eligibility

People who enter your building may or may not be eligible to borrow materials, but to ask a question at the reference desk, as a rule, they don't need to show an ID. You will need to be more explicit about eligibility for your virtual reference service, especially if you are part of a network of libraries.

Exercise 5–1. Draft a virtual reference service policy for your library regarding eligibility

Include an answer to the following question:

What is our policy regarding service to people outside our jurisdiction? (The jurisdiction of a single library system is its primary clientele; the jurisdiction of a network of libraries is the combined primary clienteles of the individual members of the network.)

Guidelines for implementing this policy should include an answer to:

How will we respond to people outside our jurisdiction who submit questions?

Confidentiality

Libraries have written policies and procedures that assure clients that their library transactions are confidential: circulation records are expunged once the borrowed material is returned; at the reference desk or on the phone, you don't ask the name of the information seeker, and when the exchange is over, there is no record of it.

In virtual reference transactions, even though the software may allow a user to ask a question anonymously, most libraries require some identification to comply with policies or regulations that limit service to primary clientele or simply to track where the questions are coming from. Unless an authenticating identifier, such as the client's library card number, is used to verify eligibility, a user can usually get away with entering a false name. Users who give a bad e-mail address, of course, forfeit the e-mailed transcript of their transaction as well as the possibility of receiving follow-up information. (One library puts the questions and answers [Q&A] of undeliverable e-mailed transcripts into a searchable file for a finite period in the hopes that the person who asked the question will find the answer.)

Virtual reference software makes it easy for you to save all of a chat transaction, including the client's identifying information. You can usually choose whether you want to keep the entire record or eliminate all or part of it. For example, you can choose to strip out clients' names and other identifiers and save only their questions and answers. Or you could save only the clients' zip codes plus the Q&A. The best of the brands allow you to have a default profile and make exceptions on a case-by-case basis. For example, when the transaction is complete, the default is to expunge the client's identifiers except for zip code and occupation, but for individual clients who give their permission, you can code the software to keep their names and other identifying information with their Q&A.

There are two prominent reasons a library would want to save the client's identifying information along with the transcript:

1. To retrieve the transcripts when helping a repeat client. Knowing the client's history of questions and answers can help you give that person better service.
2. To enable sending the client related information later. Virtual reference service is just a first step in offering personalized services, such as a current awareness service. The library may ask its clients for permission to keep a record of their transactions so that other related materials may be sent to them as they become available—similar to the services provided by online booksellers.

Many libraries choose to delete a Q&A record a few weeks after the transaction is closed. One reason for the delay in deleting the record is to allow time to edit it for inclusion in your FAQ file or knowledge base. Another is to enable a manager to review the records for quality control: to identify training needs, analyze categories of questions in order to eliminate their cause, or, in a consortium, so that one library can ensure that the answers given the clients of that library by staff in other libraries meet their satisfaction.

Exercise 5–2. Draft a virtual reference service policy for your library regarding confidentiality

Include answers to the following questions:

How long and for what purpose will we save completed transactions that include client identifiers?

Will we enable clients to give permission to save their records? If so, how will we use that information?

To the extent we keep records of clients' transactions, what is our policy with regard to handing over those records to government authorities?

Guidelines for implementing this policy should include an answer to:

What care will we take with Q&A that we edit and add to a knowledge base or FAQ file to make sure the question has been rephrased enough so that it cannot be attributable to the client who asked it?

Use of Licensed Databases to Answer Questions

The fees for use of most electronic reference databases licensed to libraries are based on the size of the libraries' primary clientele. If your virtual reference service serves people outside the boundaries of your primary clientele, however that is defined, read each licensing agreement to be sure the service complies with stipulations about who may have access to the database.

Many libraries have renegotiated their contracts with electronic database vendors specifically for providing virtual reference services. These contracts generally address the needs of a group of libraries that are networked to provide virtual reference service to their combined clientele. They might enable a librarian to answer a question (including by faxing or e-mailing a page) from a licensed database not held by the library of the questioner, or they might require that all libraries in the network subscribe if that database is to be used to answer a virtual question. For networked libraries with contracts that do not address this situation, the virtual reference system should provide a way for the answering library to know the home library of the questioner and then have access to that library's licensed databases for the purpose of answering a question.

If your library does not require verification of eligibility, you might not be able to answer a virtual reference question from a database licensed to your library.

Exercise 5–3. Draft a virtual reference service policy for your library regarding use of licensed databases

Include answers to the following questions:

What is our policy regarding answering a question from a database we subscribe to for someone outside our jurisdiction?

What is our policy about e-mailing or faxing the answer from a licensed database—to our primary clientele and to our nonprimary clientele?

Guidelines for implementing this policy should include an answer to:

How will we handle answering a question from a licensed database for someone outside our jurisdiction?

How You Will Identify Yourself to the Client

As a customer, you probably feel good when the grocery clerk calls you by your name, even though you know that information was obtained from your charge card. It is well known that addressing clients by name personalizes the transaction. (For example, "Welcome to our service, Jody." And later, "Let me know, Jody, if what I just sent you helps.") However, as the service provider, many librarians are reluctant to give their names at either the physical or virtual desk. I want to encourage you to use a personal name, which doesn't have to be your real name. From my observations of library virtual reference services, the most common practice is to give only a first name, whether real or false. Some use initials, a practice I think is far less effective because it is awkward for the client to reciprocate by calling you by your initials, so it isn't really a two-way personalized conversation. I like least the practice of giving only your title, or as in the case of a network, your title and library, as in "The Reference Librarian will be with you momentarily" or "A reference librarian at Townsville Library will be with you in a moment." Providing the client with only your title gives a cold and impersonal impression, one that is out of balance with your calling the client by name. Whatever you choose to do should be practiced by all virtual reference staff in your system.

Exercise 5–4. Draft a virtual reference policy for your library regarding how you will identify yourself to the client

Guidelines for implementing this policy should include an answer to:

Will you use your full name? The name of your library? Something else?

Delivery of Material to the Client

Virtual reference service users usually receive a record of the transaction, either the complete transcript that includes the URLs visited, or, in some cases, only the URLs visited. They obtain it either automatically via e-mail after the close of a transaction or by downloading it from the browser before the close of the transaction

> **Exercise 5–5. Draft a virtual reference service policy for your library regarding delivery of material to the client**
>
> Include answers to the following questions:
> What is our policy concerning delivery of physical materials? In particular:
>
> - Fax or mail pages from a journal? Maximum number of pages?
> - Send books via US mail? Send other physical materials, such as video tapes? Use a proxy borrower arrangement to check out the materials? Would we charge a fee for this service? If so, how much?
>
> _____
>
> Guidelines for implementing this policy should include answers to:
>
> Given our policy, how will we inform potential service users of the service?
>
> How will we respond to the clients who ask for the service? Should we offer it to those who don't ask?
>
> How will we deliver information? Photocopy and fax, or scan and fax, or scan and send as an e-mail attachment? (Supporting the policy: How handy will a photocopier or scanner be?)
>
> If a fee is charged, how will it be collected?
>
> If material is charged out and mailed to the requester, will we include a return mailer? With prepaid postage?
>
> How will we respond to a person who claims the material never arrived? Or to a person who claims it was mailed back?

(desirable when the client wishes to remain anonymous). You can understand that once clients learn about materials that answer their questions and receive some of the materials at their desktops, they expect you to be able to provide that same service, regardless of the format of those materials. In considering your policy regarding the use of licensed databases (see Exercise 5–3, page 81), you are asked to think about whether you would fax or e-mail as an attachment pages from a licensed database. In this section, you will think about the larger issue of completing the circle of finding the information to delivering it, including printed materials, sound recordings, audiotapes, and videotapes.

Average Length of Transaction

In general, virtual reference transactions take longer than those in the physical world. It takes longer to type than to say the words, and more often than at the physical desk, you tend to help the client find the answer itself rather than point to the resource that is likely to contain the answer. As your virtual reference desk gets so busy that there are clients waiting to be served, you will need to limit the amount of time you can spend with each client, just as you do at a busy desk in the library. (See Exercise 4–21 on page 73 for practice in gaining a sense of time passing in a virtual reference transaction.) It is wise to have a policy that encourages consistency among those who are staffing the virtual reference desk.

Exercise 5–6. Draft a virtual reference service policy for your library regarding average length of transaction

Include an answer to the following question:

When the virtual reference desk is busy, how long, on average, should the transaction be?
(Suggested average: 6–8 minutes or 8–12 minutes)

_____

Guidelines for implementing this policy should include answers to:

What explanation of the policy can be given to the client even before the transaction begins about what to expect given that the desk is busy?

What scripted messages will we use to indicate the policy?

What scripted messages will help to implement the policy?

Client Satisfaction

The value you place on client satisfaction should be reflected and underscored in a policy. You may need only to repeat a longstanding statement you already have. The guidelines for implementation should include the actual behaviors that achieve your goal. See Appendix 3 (pages 161 to 171) for ideas.

Exercise 5–7. Draft a virtual reference service policy for your library regarding client satisfaction

Include an answer to the following question:

In what ways does our service strive for client satisfaction? (For example: We strive to be accurate, approachable, efficient . . .; to provide personalized service; to respond promptly to complaints.)

Guidelines for implementing this policy should include answers to:

What service behaviors and system features will ensure client satisfaction (that is, What does "approachable" look like in the virtual environment?) See Appendix 3 (pages 161 to 171) for ideas about specific behaviors.

How will a client register a complaint?

Inappropriate Client Behavior

The types of problems a person can present to the staff at a virtual reference desk is more akin to those of someone calling on the telephone than to those of a person who comes to the desk. The absence of the client's physical presence limits the kinds of difficult encounters you can experience. In the chat environment, the client can behave in ways that are unreasonable or annoying to you (for example, logs on to the service repeatedly, SHOUTS at you typographically, or uses language that is objectionable to you).

Your policy with regard to such encounters should recognize that a client's anger or defensiveness may be caused by heightened frustration, which in turn was caused by an intimidating or unintuitive browser, a long wait in line, or other such setbacks initiated by the library. Also, your policy should acknowledge that with your inability to see and hear clients, you run the risk of misinterpreting their words and should encourage the staff person to initially give the benefit of the doubt to the client. (See Exercise 4–9 on page 64 for practice in responding undefensively when you are feeling unkindly toward the client.)

Exercise 5–8. Draft a virtual reference service policy for your library regarding inappropriate client behavior

Include an answer to the following question:

What constitutes inappropriate behavior or objectionable language by a virtual reference client?

Guidelines for implementing this policy should include answers to:

What scripted messages do we have for responding to a client exhibiting inappropriate behavior or using objectionable language?

Besides scripted messages, what other responses will help with a difficult client?

How should we alert potential service users about the policy? What should we say about it?

What scripted messages will we use to indicate the policy?

What action will we take with a client we deem to be mentally disturbed or threatening or who is in some other way beyond "difficult"?

Questionable Questions

Your main task here is to translate your policies about questions you don't answer into guidelines suitable to the virtual environment. Be sure you cover the three main categories of questions that you will want to be prepared to respond to with a message that conveys, "We don't answer that type of question":

- Out of scope (examples: your library doesn't collect materials on the requested topic; the staff doesn't have the expertise or the credentials for answering the question). Usual response: refer elsewhere. Several library consortia refer their virtual reference clients to a subnetwork of specialists, such as music, law, medical, genealogy, art, science, or engineering librarians. Some have lawyers, faculty in particular disciplines, doctors, or nurses on their team of experts.
- Inappropriate use of staff time (examples in some libraries: crossword puzzle definitions; contest questions; "do my homework for me" requests).
- Requests for "illegal" material (most notably, pornography, as legally defined by the community).

Exercise 5–9. Draft a virtual reference service policy for your library regarding questionable questions

Include an answer to the following question:

What categories of questions will we reject? Why?

_____

Guidelines for implementing this policy should include an answer to:

How will we respond to clients whose questions we reject? What scripted messages will we use to respond?

Limit of Transactions per Client

Because it is so easy to get to the virtual reference desk, a single client could submit so many questions that you would be spending an inordinate amount of time on the needs of that client at the expense of others. Using the same reasoning as your library's policy to limit the number of items a person can borrow in one day or the number of interlibrary loan requests a single individual can submit within a specified time frame, think about what would constitute an excessive number of virtual reference requests from one person.

Exercise 5–10. Draft a virtual reference service policy for your library regarding limit of transactions per client

Include answers to the following questions:

What, if any, is the maximum number of questions a person can ask within a specified time period?

Under what conditions will exceptions be made?

Guidelines for implementing this policy should include an answer to:

How will we respond to clients who wish to exceed the limit? What scripted messages will we use to respond?

Follow-up

Recognizing that follow-up takes time, you can either offer to do more after the close of a transaction in which you have given the client starter material, or suggest that the client return when he or she is ready for more. In the latter case, clients can be encouraged to return to the virtual reference desk or to contact you via e-mail. A policy with guidelines for implementation about follow-up will ensure that clients will receive consistent service, regardless of who is "on the desk."

Exercise 5–11. Draft a virtual reference service policy for your library regarding follow-up

Include answers to the following questions:

Under what circumstances will we initiate an offer to follow up after a transaction has ended?

Under what circumstances will we suggest clients return to the service when they are ready for more information?

Guidelines for implementing this policy should include answers to:

What scripted messages will tell the user to initiate a follow-up contact if requested?

If we promise to follow up, what checks will be put in place to ensure that it was done?

Chapter Six
Make Your Virtual Reference Desk a Comfortable Place

Just as your physical desk has a personality that falls somewhere along the spectrum from inviting to intimidating, so too can your cyberdesk range from welcoming to bewildering. But unlike at the physical desk, you do not have the opportunity at the cyberdesk to counteract with your friendly face the negative message conveyed by an unapproachable setting. In the library, the client's mood can be shaped by an intimidating entrance to the library; by a too-quiet reading room with courtroom-high ceilings; or by a bar-height reference counter that says, "I can't spend much time with you" or "We deal only with questions that have quick answers." Similarly, at the virtual desk, a client may feel daunted by a busy Web page dense with text, confused by jargon or ambiguously worded instructions, or stupid because a poorly designed Web page doesn't give an instant sense of what's happening now and what to do next. Clients who have an off-putting introduction to your virtual service may get discouraged and never ask the question, might not stick with you throughout the transaction, and will likely not return.

Develop Homepage Features That Encourage Access

The simpler your homepage is, visually and textually, the less time a person needs to spend figuring it out. If it takes more than 30 seconds to pick out the sought-after information or link, the searcher, especially someone new to your site, is likely to give up.

To help ensure a positive first impression of your site, consider the following ten basic principles of effective Web page design of a site's homepage or any entry point of a major subsection of a site. It would be hard to design a homepage that would get a perfect score. Library sites are sufficiently complex and their users so diverse that some compromises are necessary, but it is important to try to get as close as you can to a welcoming and engaging entry to your service.

Designing accessible Web pages for people with disabilities

For help in designing user-friendly Web space for people with disabilities, visit the following resources:

Valle Verde Library at El Paso Community College
http://www.epcc.edu/vvlib/webada.htm
and
EASI (Equal Access to Software and Information) at Rochester Institute of Technology
http://www.rit.edu/~easi/access.htm
and
Trace Research & Development Center University of Wisconsin–Madison
http://trace.wisc.edu/world/web/

Figures 6–1 and 6–2 show two homepages that I believe do a good job of adhering to the principles. Following these examples of homepages that work well is an exercise that asks you to evaluate a few libraries' homepage screens. (My apologies to the libraries whose Web pages are shown as needing improvement. This is one time when I would be happy to learn that the page shown here is out of date!)

You'll find more guidelines for effective Web sites in Chapter Eight (pages 138 to 145).

Top ten basic principles of Web homepage design

1. Design an uncluttered page. Leave lots of blank space around and between logical sections.

2. Keep text to a minimum. Review what you've written and strike out all superfluous words. Be consistent in spelling terms, especially Web vs. web; e-mail vs. email; online vs. on-line or on line. Know when to spell "library" with an uppercase or lowercase *L*.

3. Make your homepage fit within the bounds of a single screen (no vertical or horizontal scrolling necessary). Bear in mind that a range of different browsers, screen sizes, and font sizes are used by your clients.

4. For the most frequently used functions, enable users to get the results they are looking for in one or two clicks of the mouse. For example, by displaying on your homepage three search boxes, each with a drop-down menu of choices, you could make it possible for a user at the homepage to enter a term for searching the catalog by author, title, subject, etc.; enter a term to search for an article by database; or enter a query to submit to your reference service by e-mail or live chat. In Figure 6–1, notice that you can enter terms for searching the online catalog directly from the homepage.

Another way to keep to a minimum the number of layers a user must pass through is by using mouse-over pop-up links to all functions subsumed under the homepage link that is pointed to, as shown in Figure 6–2.

5. Avoid long, unbroken lists. Choices beyond four or five are unlikely to be read (exception: A browsable index, extraction from an index, or other lists in alphabetical, chronological, call number, relevancy, or other order that the searcher recognizes as coherent).

Figure 6–1 Example of enabling retrieval of desired results directly from the homepage of the Yale University Library (www.library. yale.edu)

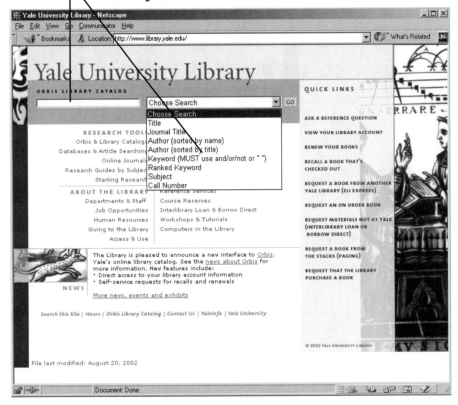

Search box and drop-down menu of online catalog search options

6. Use typography and color to guide the eye, not confuse it.

7. Use images sparingly, and ones that support the topic they relate to. Keep the file sizes of images small so a searcher doesn't have a long wait (more than a couple of seconds can seem long) while it loads onto the browser.

8. Use parallel construction of lists. Drop "-ing" from verb endings. For example:

Poor	Better (parallel construction)	Even better (dropped "-ing")
How to get a library card	Getting a library card	Get a library card
Searching the catalog	Searching the catalog	Search the catalog
Reference services	Accessing reference services	Access reference services

(For "Best," see next principle)

9. Clearly label links. Don't require users to guess which link to put their cursor on to get the pop-up explanation of where that link goes. To cover bases, however, use mouse-over definitions that pop up as links are pointed to. Even better, when the cur-

Figure 6–2 Homepage of the University of Nevada Las Vegas Libraries showing mouse-over pop-up links to subcategories of a main link (www.library.unlv.edu)

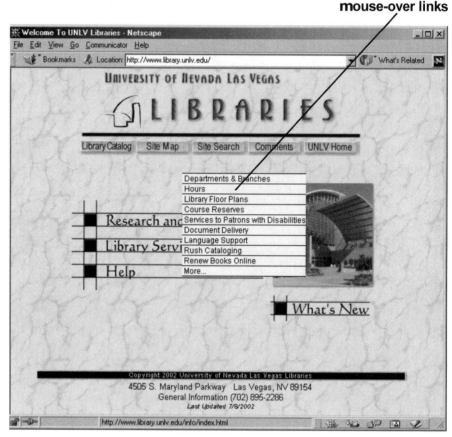

sor is over a link, have both the definition of the link appear as well as pop-up sublinks. Most important, provide choices from the user's standpoint, not from the library's standpoint. Continuing with the example in #8:

Best

Get a library card

Find a book or article

Ask a question

10. Avoid jargon; if you must use it, be sure to define it. Library technical terminology is filled with common words, such as "catalog" or "reference," that mean something quite different when used as everyday language. For example, "catalog" for a surprising number of library users is not at all a clear concept. Some conjure up the image of a Sears-type catalog, others, the campus course catalog. Test the vocabulary on your Web site by having your users tell you how they interpret it.

Library homepages that work

Figures 6–3 and 6–4 (a and b) are my choices of homepages that come closest to meeting all ten principles of Web homepage design, followed by a scorecard of my specific rankings on each principle.

Figure 6–3 Homepage of the University of Nevada Las Vegas Libraries (www.library.unlv.edu)

Exercises in evaluating library homepages

The examples used in exercises 6–1 through 6–10 are library homepages that, in my opinion, have a mixture of effective and flawed features and would benefit from a stricter adherence to the design principles. In some cases, the site represents an individual library organization; in other cases, it represents a consortium of libraries. In every case, the library or consortium offers a question-answering service of some type, whether by phone, post, e-mail, or Web (in one case, the homepage is that of a virtual reference service of a networked library). In these exercises, you are asked for your opinions on several design issues.

Figure 6–4a **Homepage of the Charlotte & Mecklenburg County Library (www.plcmc.lib.nc.us)**

Figure 6–4b **Charlotte & Mecklenburg County Library: same homepage showing rotating centerpieces. The center space is also used for mouse-over definitions of links.**

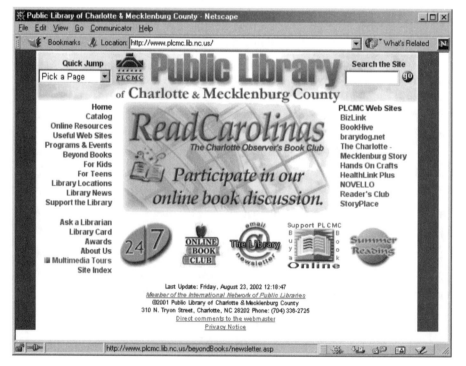

Anne's Scorecard for Figures 6–3 and 6–4 (a & b)

☑ = mostly or fully satisfies criterion
± = partially satisfies criterion
❑ = does not satisfy criterion

Figure 6–3 (with 6–2)	Figures 6–4a and 6–4b
☑ Uncluttered	☑ Uncluttered
☑ No text overload	☑ No text overload
☑ No scrolling needed	☑ No scrolling needed
± Results one click away	± Results one click away
☑ Length of lists: short	❑ Length of lists: short
☑ Typography and colors help, not hinder	☑ Typography and colors help, not hinder
☑ Spare use of images	☑ Spare use of images
☑ "Parallel" list construction	☑ "Parallel" list construction
☑ Clearly labeled links	☑ Clearly labeled links
☑ Jargon-free	☑ Jargon-free

Note: Because of the small size of the screen as reproduced here, the libraries' URLs are included so that you view the screen on your computer. However, because it is likely the site now has a different look, be prepared to evaluate the changed screen.

Instructions for Exercise 6–1 through 6–10

Step 1. Examine each of the screens in Exercises 6–1 through 6–10. Imagine that you are visiting each site, and answer the questions that follow each screen.

Step 2. When you have completed these exercises, look over your library's homepage. Try to view it from the standpoint of a naive user, and answer the following questions:

a. What would a first-time visitor think of the page?

b. How obvious is the way to ask a reference question?

c. How would you improve it?

d. What specifically do you like about it that you want to keep?

e. What specifically about it do you want to change?

f. On a scale of 1–10 (10=user friendliest), how would you rank your library's homepage?

Exercise 6–1. Evaluate the homepage of the University of California, Berkeley, Library

Homepage of the University of California, Berkeley, Library (www.lib.berkeley.edu)

Homepage design principles	
__ Uncluttered	What is your first impression of the page?
__ No text overload	_____
__ No scrolling needed	How obvious is the way to ask a reference question?
__ Results one click away	_____
__ Length of lists: short	How would you improve it?_____
__ Typography and colors help, not hinder	_____
__ Spare use of images	What specifically do you like about it that you would want to emulate?
__ "Parallel" list construction	_____
__ Clearly labeled links	What specifically about it would you want to avoid?
__ Jargon-free	_____
	On a scale of 1–10 (10=user-friendliest), how would you rank this site?_____

Exercise 6–2. Evaluate the homepage of Hawaii State Public Library System

Homepage of Hawaii State Public Library System (www.hcc.hawaii.edu/hspls)

Homepage design principles	
__ Uncluttered	What is your first impression of the page?
__ No text overload	_____
__ No scrolling needed	How obvious is the way to ask a reference question?
__ Results one click away	_____
__ Length of lists: short	How would you improve it?_____
__ Typography and colors help, not hinder	_____
__ Spare use of images	What specifically do you like about it that you would want to emulate?
__ "Parallel" list construction	_____
__ Clearly labeled links	What specifically about it would you want to avoid?
__ Jargon-free	_____
	On a scale of 1–10 (10=user-friendliest), how would you rank this site?_____

Exercise 6–3. Evaluate the homepage of networked academic libraries in the Illinois Alliance Library System

Homepage of networked academic libraries in the Illinois Alliance Library System
(www.alliancelibrarysystem.com/Projects/ReadyRef/index.html)

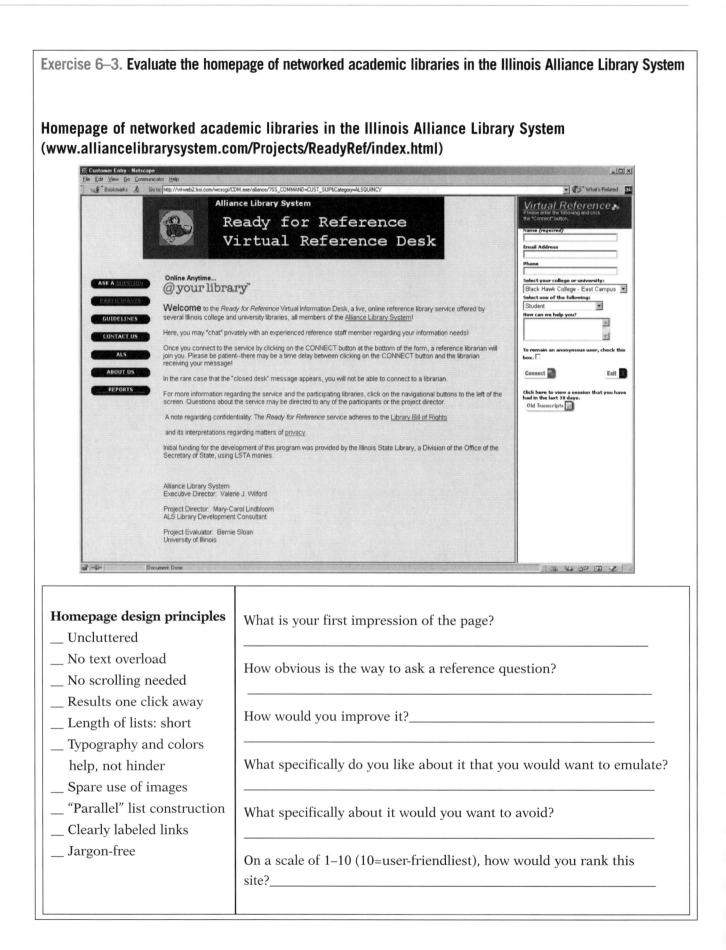

Homepage design principles
__ Uncluttered
__ No text overload
__ No scrolling needed
__ Results one click away
__ Length of lists: short
__ Typography and colors
   help, not hinder
__ Spare use of images
__ "Parallel" list construction
__ Clearly labeled links
__ Jargon-free

What is your first impression of the page?
_____

How obvious is the way to ask a reference question?
_____

How would you improve it?_____
_____

What specifically do you like about it that you would want to emulate?
_____

What specifically about it would you want to avoid?
_____

On a scale of 1–10 (10=user-friendliest), how would you rank this site?_____

Exercise 6–4. Evaluate the homepage of the Cambridge University Library

Homepage of the Cambridge University Library (www.lib.cam.ac.uk)

Homepage design principles	
__ Uncluttered	What is your first impression of the page?
__ No text overload	_____
__ No scrolling needed	How obvious is the way to ask a reference question?
__ Results one click away	_____
__ Length of lists: short	How would you improve it?_____
__ Typography and colors help, not hinder	_____
__ Spare use of images	What specifically do you like about it that you would want to emulate?
__ "Parallel" list construction	_____
__ Clearly labeled links	What specifically about it would you want to avoid?
__ Jargon-free	_____
	On a scale of 1–10 (10=user-friendliest), how would you rank this site?_____

Exercise 6–5. Evaluate the homepage of the New Haven Free Public Library

Homepage of the New Haven Free Public Library (www.nhfpl.lib.ct.us)

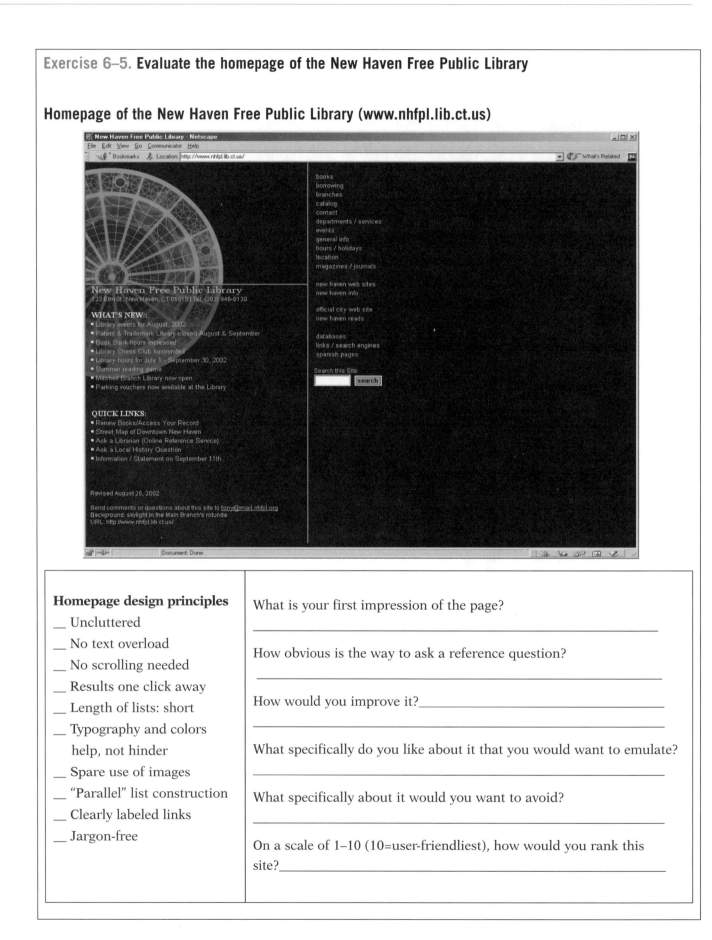

Homepage design principles

__ Uncluttered

__ No text overload

__ No scrolling needed

__ Results one click away

__ Length of lists: short

__ Typography and colors help, not hinder

__ Spare use of images

__ "Parallel" list construction

__ Clearly labeled links

__ Jargon-free

What is your first impression of the page?

_____

How obvious is the way to ask a reference question?

_____

How would you improve it?_____

_____

What specifically do you like about it that you would want to emulate?

_____

What specifically about it would you want to avoid?

_____

On a scale of 1–10 (10=user-friendliest), how would you rank this site?_____

Exercise 6–6. Evaluate the homepage of the Iowa City Public Library

Homepage of the Iowa City Public Library (www.iowa-city.lib.ia.us)

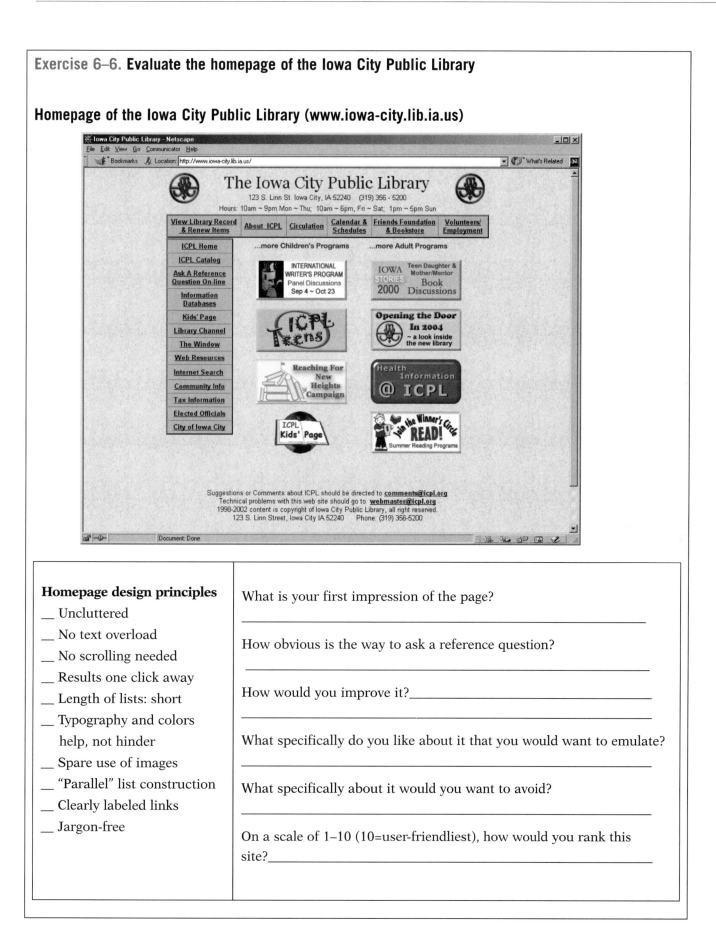

Homepage design principles	
__ Uncluttered	What is your first impression of the page?
__ No text overload	_____
__ No scrolling needed	How obvious is the way to ask a reference question?
__ Results one click away	_____
__ Length of lists: short	
__ Typography and colors	How would you improve it?_____
help, not hinder	_____
__ Spare use of images	What specifically do you like about it that you would want to emulate?
__ "Parallel" list construction	_____
__ Clearly labeled links	What specifically about it would you want to avoid?
__ Jargon-free	_____
	On a scale of 1–10 (10=user-friendliest), how would you rank this site?_____

Exercise 6–7. Evaluate the homepage of Santa Monica Public Library

Homepage of Santa Monica Public Library (www.smpl.org)

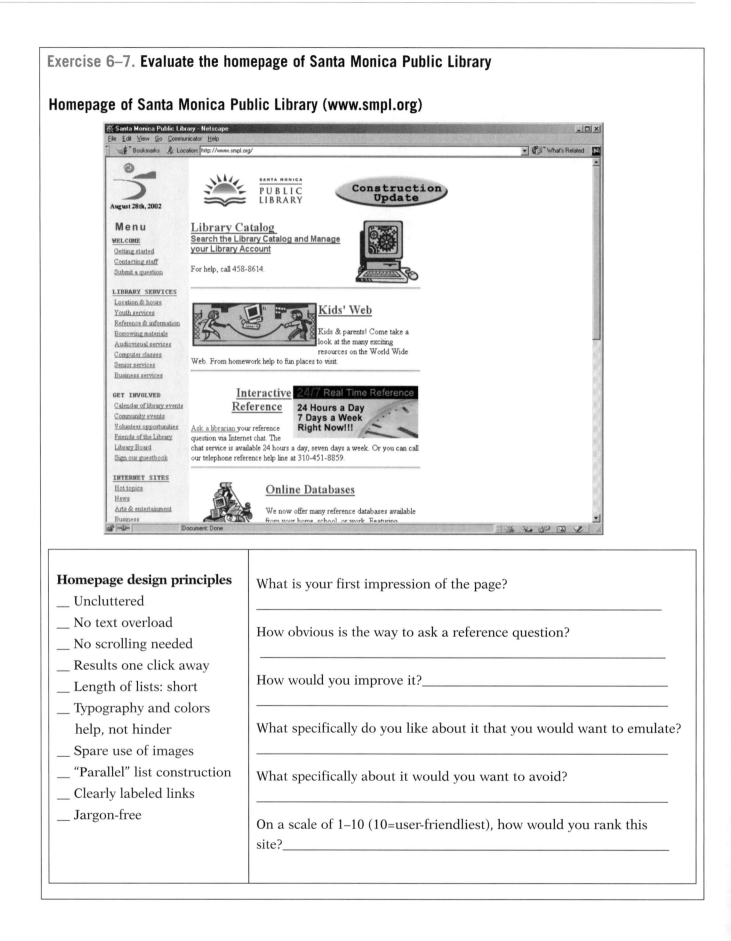

Homepage design principles

__ Uncluttered

__ No text overload

__ No scrolling needed

__ Results one click away

__ Length of lists: short

__ Typography and colors help, not hinder

__ Spare use of images

__ "Parallel" list construction

__ Clearly labeled links

__ Jargon-free

What is your first impression of the page?

_____

How obvious is the way to ask a reference question?

_____

How would you improve it?_____

_____

What specifically do you like about it that you would want to emulate?

_____

What specifically about it would you want to avoid?

_____

On a scale of 1–10 (10=user-friendliest), how would you rank this site?_____

Exercise 6–8. Evaluate the homepage of the Princeton University Library

Homepage of the Princeton University Library (http://libweb.princeton.edu)

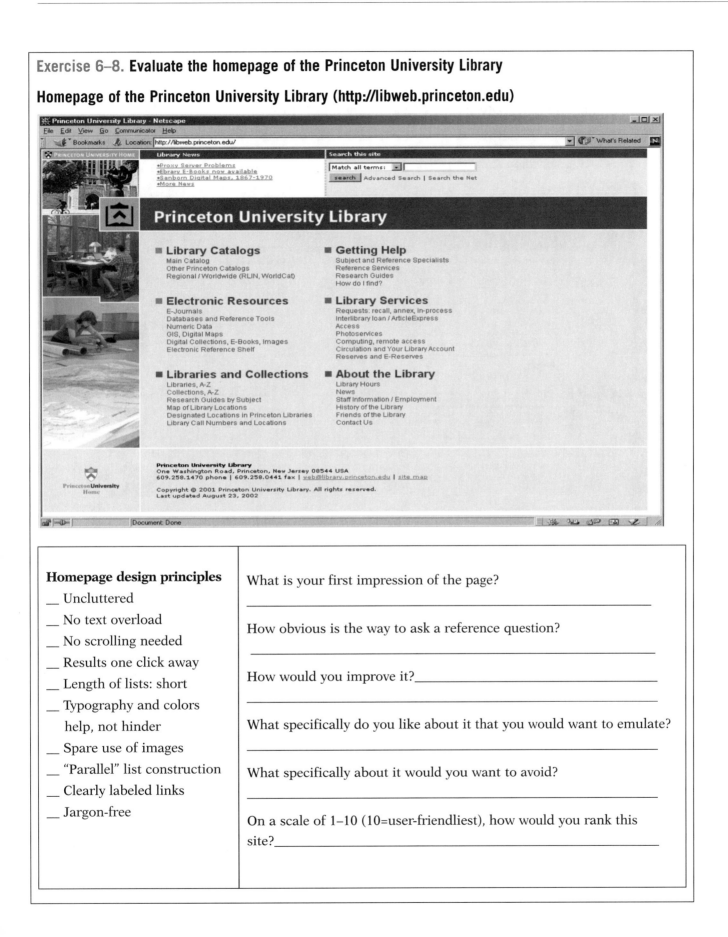

Homepage design principles	
__ Uncluttered	What is your first impression of the page?
__ No text overload	_____
__ No scrolling needed	How obvious is the way to ask a reference question?
__ Results one click away	_____
__ Length of lists: short	How would you improve it?_____
__ Typography and colors help, not hinder	_____
__ Spare use of images	What specifically do you like about it that you would want to emulate?
__ "Parallel" list construction	_____
__ Clearly labeled links	What specifically about it would you want to avoid?
__ Jargon-free	_____
	On a scale of 1–10 (10=user-friendliest), how would you rank this site?_____

Exercise 6–9. Evaluate the homepage of the Yale University Library

Homepage of the Yale University Library (www.library.yale.edu)

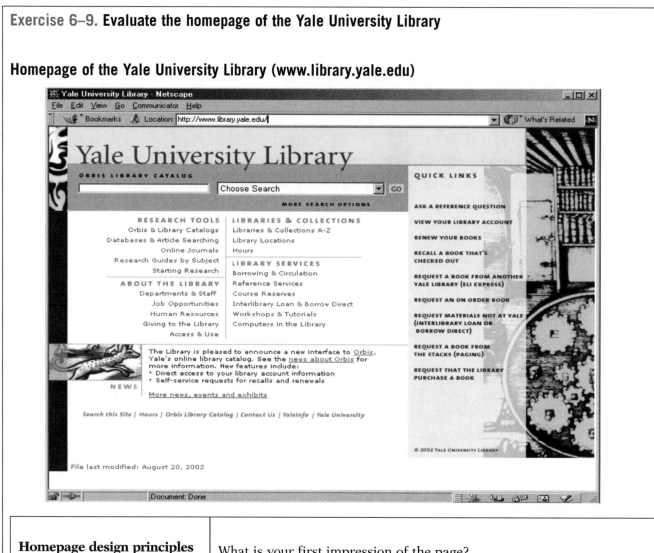

Homepage design principles

__ Uncluttered

__ No text overload

__ No scrolling needed

__ Results one click away

__ Length of lists: short

__ Typography and colors
   help, not hinder

__ Spare use of images

__ "Parallel" list construction

__ Clearly labeled links

__ Jargon-free

What is your first impression of the page?

_____

How obvious is the way to ask a reference question?

_____

How would you improve it?_____

_____

What specifically do you like about it that you would want to emulate?

_____

What specifically about it would you want to avoid?

_____

On a scale of 1–10 (10=user-friendliest), how would you rank this site?_____

Exercise 6–10. Evaluate the homepage of Vassar College Libraries

Homepage of Vassar College Libraries (http://library.vassar.edu)

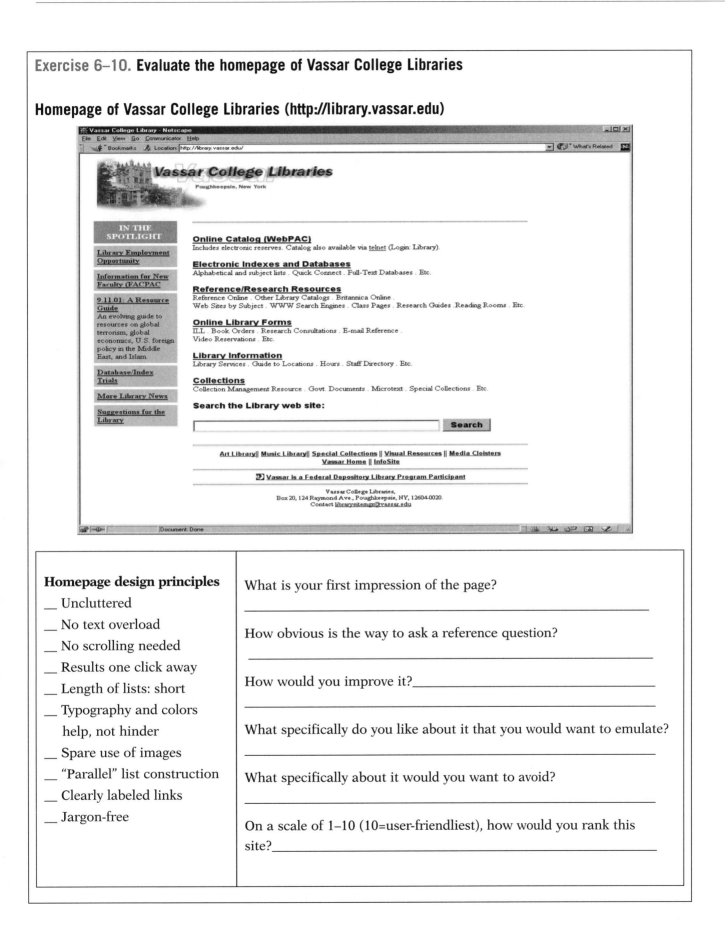

Homepage design principles	
__ Uncluttered	What is your first impression of the page?
__ No text overload	_____
__ No scrolling needed	How obvious is the way to ask a reference question?
__ Results one click away	_____
__ Length of lists: short	How would you improve it?_____
__ Typography and colors	_____
help, not hinder	
__ Spare use of images	What specifically do you like about it that you would want to emulate?
__ "Parallel" list construction	_____
__ Clearly labeled links	What specifically about it would you want to avoid?
__ Jargon-free	_____
	On a scale of 1–10 (10=user-friendliest), how would you rank this site?_____

Plan the Look and Feel of Your Virtual Reference Service

The following list is neither exhaustive nor prescriptive, but rather is intended, together with the exercises on pages 109 to 118 as a springboard for your discussions, planning, and decisions about the look of various screens, their content, and links. It is especially important that collaborating library systems agree on these basic issues. Get ideas by seeing how other libraries have dealt with them.

Also, see Chapter Eight (pages 138 to 145) for additional criteria for and examples of effective Web sites.

Decisions to make when planning your Web site

Routes to the virtual reference service
Representation on collaborating member libraries' homepages
First impressions
Who is eligible to use the service?
Clients' expectations
Your expertise
Related services
"Wait, please" screen
Client satisfaction
"Staff only" screens

Exercise 6–11. **Routes to the virtual reference service**

How does the client enter the service? Decide the route(s) a client could take to ask a question. For example:

- Direct access to the service site
- Library homepage → service
- All pages of the Web catalog → service
- Web sites throughout the community that have links to the service

– –

Notes and decisions

Exercise 6–12. Representation on collaborating member libraries' homepages

Decide what will appear about the service when the client accesses the local library's Web site.

For example: The Santa Monica Public Library is one member of a consortium of libraries networked to provide virtual reference service. Visit that library's homepage (www.smpl.org). Notice how their interactive reference service is described. Then click on Interactive Reference to get to the consortium page and compare.

— —

Notes and decisions

Exercise 6–13. **First impressions**

What will clients see when they get to the homepage of the service?

Decide whether and where the following will go on the homepage (and, if not on the homepage, where?):

- Logo
- Welcome message
- About the service
- Search box for inputting a query
- Authentication input box
- When we're not open . . .
- Links to other pages, such as What to expect, Hours of service, Who we are, Where we are, Related services

For textual information, decide whether the full text itself or only a link to it should be on the homepage.

— —

Notes and decisions

Exercise 6–14. Who is eligible to use the service?

If you limit service to your primary clientele, decide what information you will require for verifying their eligibility. A good arrangement is one in which users pick an ID and password, or anything else that is easy to memorize. If you simply want demographic information about your users, decide what information you'll request and how you'll ask for it.

Notes and decisions

Exercise 6–15. **Clients' expectations**

Decide here the text that explains the service to the client, and where that explanation will be located.

Notes and decisions

Exercise 6–16. Your expertise

Here is where you have the opportunity to describe how your service differs from a commercial reference service; for example, staff credentials, resources consulted, service values (reliable information, no ads, no rigged relevancy rankings, sources are cited), part of a global network.

_____

Notes and decisions

Exercise 6–17. **Related services**

Decide here what other services the client should know about, either as alternatives to the virtual reference service (such as e-mail and phone service, non-English-language service) or as supplements to it (such as a document delivery service, current awareness service, research assistance, specialized information services, instructional services, fee services).

Notes and decisions

Exercise 6–18. "Wait, please" screen

Decide on a screen that could be sent to clients to fill time while they wait as you search for answers. Consider providing choices; for example, library news, world news, weather, search engines.

Notes and decisions

Exercise 6–19. Client satisfaction

Decide here the content of the request for clients' evaluation of the service, and when and how it should be shown to the client. (See suggestions on page 120.)

Notes and decisions

Exercise 6–20. "Staff only" screens

Consider putting useful information for staff on the virtual reference site, accessible by staff only. The benefit is centralized information that is easy to update and that staff can routinely check or be alerted to check when new information is posted. Topics might include:

- profiles of participating libraries
- service policies and guidelines
- calendar of desk duty assignments

Notes and decisions

Listen to the Evaluations of Your Users

Regardless of how good the final version of your Web site looks to you, you will need to get the perspective of a sampling of your users. To the extent your site doesn't work for them, accept that as true and try to figure out what to change and how to change it to make it work. Regularly analyze your users' complaints and make changes to eliminate them. You will need to change either the design feature that is a problem or the users' expectations when they use that feature. Following are three methods of soliciting your users' evaluations.

Usability studies

The following exercises will give you practice in various techniques for determining the degree of user-friendliness of your service.

Exercise 6–21. Observe users as they use your Web site

1. Recruit users for a specified amount of time.
2. Observe them using your site as naturally as possible, asking their own questions, and in the location where they normally search: at a library computer, at home, at the office.
3. Ask users to think out loud as they search. Listen for how they name the categories they want to use and how they interpret the choices your Web site gives them, e.g., "Think aloud" would indicate "catalog" is misunderstood: "I'm hoping to find information about how to raise fish. I'll click on Catalogs, to find a fisherman's catalog. Oops, didn't work. I'll try Ask a librarian . . . ."
4. Take notes. If given permission, record the users' think-aloud comments.
5. Offer to share your observations with the users after they have completed their searches.
6. Give study participants a reward or thank-you gift.

Post-transaction evaluation form

Provide an easy-to-use, *short* evaluation form. The form should fit within the boundaries of one screen, and should encourage users to tell what they liked and didn't like about using your service.

Suggested questions for a post-transaction short form:

- **Have you used this service before? If yes, how many times? [Provide ranges of choices; e.g., once or twice, once a week, once a month, more frequently.]**
- **If this is your first time using this service, how did you hear about it? [Try letting the responder answer freely, without providing multiple choices.]**
- **How helpful was the service you received today? (check one)**

  ❑ Very helpful　　　❑ Helpful ❑　　　Not so helpful

  Comments:

- **Any suggestions for improving this service?**
- **What I would really like to say about using this service is:**

Meetings with your users

From time to time, meet with groups of clients who use the service to talk about what works, what doesn't, and what new features they would like to see on your Web site and your virtual reference service. The meeting may be an informal gathering or a more formal focus group. If the latter, to get usable results, you will need to conform to the guidelines of conducting focus groups. The advantage to the former is that you can spend less time preparing the issues for discussion and soliciting appropriate participants, but you should expect the results to be more intuitive than objectively representative.

Exercise 6–22. Observe users as they use your Web site on your terms

1. Recruit users for a specified amount of time.
2. Ask users to conduct a search on a question you have prepared. You may conduct this study anywhere that is mutually acceptable where you can easily observe as they search.
3. You may ask them to think out loud (as in Exercise 6–21), or you may simply observe as they search in silence. In either case, you want to compare what you expected them to do to what they actually do.
4. To record your observations, use a form that enables you to check off search actions and strategies that were performed as you expected, thus limiting your note-taking to what went wrong or differently.
5. Offer to share your observations with the users after they have completed their searches.
6. Give study participants a reward or thank-you gift.

Exercise 6–23. Analyze transaction logs

1. Check your transaction logs regularly for failures. Examine error messages, zero retrievals, humongous retrievals, and examples of trying different strategies in vain in the logs of your electronic databases and Web site usage. Notice where users are repeatedly going wrong and work to fix it.

2. Analyze the scripts of your virtual reference transactions, regarding each question as evidence of the failure of your Web site to help clients find what was needed on their own. Categorize the questions and work away at solutions that would reduce or eliminate them.

Part 3
Building a Lively Service

Your library no doubt proudly proclaims its mission of serving the diverse needs of the entire community. It probably comes closest to fulfilling this promise in relation to the children in your jurisdiction. This section is intended to help you move your library closer to fulfilling its mission to the adult community. To the extent you follow the advice in the next two chapters, you may achieve a desired objective or two (service to a larger portion of your community; increased use of the library, its resources, and services, including by heretofore nonusers). But your success may create a new problem: overload. It is the kind of problem any commercial business would welcome, and it is my hope that you would welcome it, too. So be warned: Skip this part altogether if you don't want to test the limits of how much business you can handle.

Chapter Seven
Market and Publicize the Service in Old and New Ways

The business world makes an important distinction between marketing and selling that is blurred in library language. In business, marketing refers to the process of generating the prospect of sales by determining what's needed by past *and* potential *customers and figuring out products or services that meet those needs; selling is the process of encouraging people to buy an existing product or service, regardless of whether it best meets their needs. When libraries use the word "marketing," they usually mean publicizing their existing services to their community. In this chapter, "marketing" and "publicizing" are subsumed under the term "promoting," on the premise that librarians are in a good position to combine the two concepts: to listen to their users for the purpose of fulfilling needs that are not correctly addressed in the course of or as a consequence of publicizing the service.*

Since at least the mid-1980s, we have been saying, "We should do a better job of marketing [or publicizing] the library." But too many libraries seem unable to get past the "should" stage. The thinking underlying the inertia must go something like this:

There are no consequences if we keep things as they are. The library—whether public or academic—is such a valued symbol of democracy and lifelong learning, we can take for granted that it, and therefore we, will always be here. (School and special libraries know how fragile their status can be.)

or

We waged a one-shot publicity campaign, saw a spike in use, which was followed by back-to-the-usual traffic, and we didn't have the energy or money to mount other such drives.

or

We're busy enough and don't have the resources to handle more, so while we're aware of the large numbers in our jurisdiction we don't serve, we'd better not try to raise expectations we can't fulfill.

Today, many of the libraries that have launched virtual reference services to serve their clientele in new ways think differently. They see negative consequences to continuing business as usual. They observe the influence of commercial sales techniques and try to emulate them by energetically publicizing their services to people both inside and outside the library. They keep one eye on their disappearing users and the nonusers in their community to learn what new services the library should offer that would meet their information needs. And they manage the resulting increase in business by forging alliances with reference staff in other libraries to share the load.

Four essential strategies can be used to promote your service:

1. Create a general awareness of the service.
2. Segment the market.
3. Ask users how they heard about your service.
4. Keep up with your community's changing information needs.

You need to undertake all four to be successful.

Strategy 4 focuses on pure marketing techniques. In strategies 1 through 3, the marketing part of each strategy begins when someone uses your service to ask a question to which your answer is some form of no. (For example, "You are eligible to use this service, but we don't answer such questions" or "We don't provide the service you expected.") At that moment, you ask yourself, "What need was being expressed that we don't fill? How could we turn the response to such questions into a yes?"

Example: Imagine that at the virtual reference desk you sent to the caller Web pages and full texts of articles from your databases of electronic journals. Also, in the course of walking the caller through the process of finding materials in your print collection via your online catalog, you point out a book that is on topic, and you ensure the caller that its bibliographic details will be sent in the e-mailed transcript of the session.

Caller: Thanks! Could you please send me the book?

You: Sorry, you'll need to come to the library to get it. Would you like to know our hours?
[Your marketer's mind turns on, notes the caller's desire for convenient service, and asks, "What would it take to be able to send the caller the book? How can the barriers be removed to make it possible to say yes to such questions?"]

Regardless of the strategy you use, *always* designate the *librarian*, not the library, as the provider of the service. "Librarian" combines both the human and expert contact that the client is seeking.

Promotion Strategy 1: Create Awareness

The greater the awareness of your service, the greater the number who use it. More specifically, the more people who know about your service, *including people who do not need it or use it*, the more people will use it when their need arises. Or, you can look at it this way: If you are talking only to people with whom you are already in touch, you are missing the many who would use your service if they were conscious of its existence. If you are doing it right, a surveyor could theoretically ask every member of your constituency if they are aware of your service, regardless of whether they have used it, and the overwhelming response should be in the affirmative.

This shallow awareness—"I know the service exists, but I don't necessarily know anything specific about it"—is achieved by blitzing your community with memorable slogans, your logo, and little else. Your aim is to convey in a few words and a picture only three particulars:

- the name of your service
- why the service should be used
- how to reach the service

Here are five ways to create a general awareness of your virtual reference service. Implementing only one of them won't do much. The sustained, in-your-face (meaning impossible to ignore) use of a variety of approaches will make a difference.

1. Devise a catchy slogan or simply stated message, and plant it everywhere you can think of.

    Examples of slogans:
    - **This About.com's advertisement appeared on the sides of New York City's buses:**
      Q: Who? What? When? Where? Why?
      Answer: About.com
    - **Infopeople's slogan**
      Your best Internet connection is your librarian [followed by a URL, or, on the Internet, a link]
    - **Others (Anne-made)**
      When Google isn't working, your librarian is.
      or

When Jeeves doesn't get it, ask a librarian.
　　or
Question authority: your reference librarian.
　　or
Want the RIGHT answer? Ask a librarian.

Regardless of the slogan you choose, wherever it appears it should be followed by a URL, or, on the Internet, a link to your Web site.

2. Design an eye-catching, self-explanatory logo and use it (with your slogan) everywhere you talk about your service. Examples of effective logos:

- QandAcafe: The chat reference service of California's public libraries in the San Francisco Bay Area

- QuestionPoint: The global reference service spearheaded by the Library of Congress and OCLC

- KnowItNow24x7: The CLEVNET Library Consortium

- 24/7 Reference: The collaborative service sponsored by the Metropolitan Cooperative Library System, based in California

- Virtual Information Desk: A network of academic libraries in Pennsylvania

3. Give away useful promotional items that include your logo and URL.

Examples of giveaways:

- A decorative reminder of your service that can be mounted with Velcro on one's personal computer, distributed at a table outside your local grocery store or the student union.
- A paper bookmark, inserted in discharged books and in books sold at your local bookstore, about how to put a shortcut to your service on one's desktop or a direct link to your service on the personal toolbar of one's browser.
- Stickers, which can be put on a telephone or in an address book, that describe different ways to reach to a library help desk; include these in the library's mass mailings.

4. Maintain a presence in your local media.

Write a regular column for your local newspaper, your utilities bill insert, or your quarterly library newsletter (if you have one). Use it as an opportunity to show how to get results on the Internet or by using other electronic resources. Don't just say, for example, "To use this marvelous service, just go to [URL] and click on Ask a librarian. Then follow the directions on the screen." For too many adults, that isn't sufficient information to motivate them to try it out. Show the step-by-step process. Figure 7–1 is an example of good writing from the client's standpoint, and Figure 7–2 is an example of clear instructions (both are from a newsletter of the Belvedere-Tiburon Library, a public library in California).

5. Make it easy for surfers to find you.

"Publicizing in the context of the Web," says Jeffrey Beall, "means ensuring that your site gets adequately indexed in the appropriate search engines." His article tells you how to increase the likelihood that anyone searching for information you have created and published on the Web will find you. For your virtual reference service, if you followed all the ways he suggests, you might be deluged with people who are not eligible for your service. However, by choosing search engines that are internal to the sites whose users you want to attract, you can somewhat control the number and eligibility of the people who stumble upon you. Beall suggests that "the most successful way to get your Web site included in the search engines is to visit their home pages, look for the 'Add URL' button (or equivalent), click on it, and follow the instructions." (Beall,

Figure 7–1 Example of an article about the service written from the client's standpoint

"Move Over, Google ..."

"... Make way, Yahoo. Meet Lynn, the live online reference librarian." That's what the San Jose Mercury News headlined its story last March when Bay Area Libraries launched the Q and A Cafe, a question-answering service that "matches the speed of search engines with the smarts of librarians."

If you haven't yet used the service, you might be settling for less than the best when searching for answers to your questions. Two Belvedere-Tiburon residents share their experiences at the Q and A Cafe:

BW: "It was after dinner; my son's homework, a paper on the Bucky Ball, was due the next day for his honors geometry class. We spent at least an hour looking on our shelves and on the Internet. Then we tried QandAcafe, and within 5 minutes we had the answer! The librarian didn't just say "check this or that place"; she gave us the answer. Now the Cafe is our first choice to go to when we're stuck."

CA: In a book I was reading, I came to a couplet in French, a language I don't know. So I asked QandAcafe. The librarian went to the French Consulate for a translation and sent it to me. Great service!

Other comments the Library has received:

"The most thorough service I've experienced!"

"The librarian was very professional and answered my questions quickly and thoroughly."

"You're my new favorite librarian!"

"I was thrilled to get your emailed transcript of our conversation, with the Web addresses of the sites you took me to!"

How does the service work? See "The Q & A Cafe is 5 steps away" [Figure 7–2] for step-by-step instructions.

Reprinted with permission from *In the Stacks* (Belvedere-Tiburon Library newsletter), February 2002

Figure 7–2 Example of publicizing the service by showing how to use it

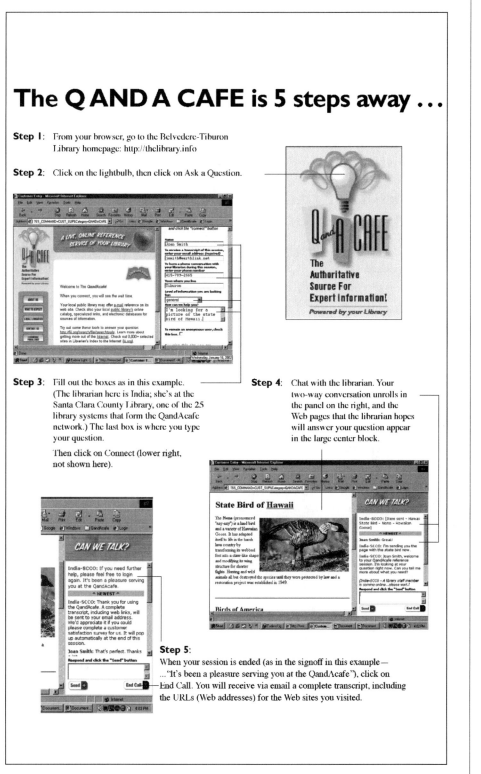

1998: 160–162) To limit those who find you to members of your city or campus community, add your URL (if it isn't already there) to the homepage of your parent organization or other organization whose site is visited by people you want to attract. Then, be sure that the text on your homepage uses words that are likely to be used by a searcher. (Search engines look for matches on words, so don't rely on a graphic to represent your message; add text to the graphic.) In that way, only people putting keywords into a "search this site" option (or its equivalent) will find you.

Promotion Strategy 2: Segment the Market

Children's and young adult librarians understand that there are different stages of childhood and that in each stage, children have separate needs. Storyhours for toddlers are different from storyhours for preschoolers, and homework help is offered to the older kids but not to the ones too young to have homework. Advice about good reading is different for preteens than it is for the 12 to 16-year-olds. We tend to treat adults, however, as if they stopped growing and changing once they reached age 21. Except for services targeted to different language groups, where the need for materials in their languages is obvious, library services to adults are reduced to one size fits all. In fact, adults can be separated into groups with special interests and needs, depending on age, work, cultural background, and so on. The business world addresses these different needs by "segmenting the market," which translates to:

> Don't tell your potential clients what you can offer them; tell them that their need (which you specify) can be satisfied by your service. Then position your service to fulfill that need.

To take this approach, you need to know your clients' information needs and how to articulate them so they will be recognized. In a segmented approach, it is quite possible to provide the same service to an entire population, but call the service by different names and use different examples to describe the service, depending on which segment you are talking to.

For example, a university library offers round-the-clock virtual reference service to the campus community. Instead of one message to everyone ("Got a question at 2:00 A.M.? Ask a librarian."), here are some messages directed to subsets of that community:

To lower-division students (sent to dorms at exams time):

> "Up all night cramming and stuck for some information? Our 24/7 quick-fact experts await your cybercall."

To upper-division students (sent to campus departments and student advisers to post):

> "Can't sleep? Need a good quotation for the speech you have to give in tomorrow's seminar? A librarian can help."

> "Stuck in the midst of writing your term paper? Try our 24/7 term paper advisory experts."

To graduate students (sent to graduate schools to post):

> "Having trouble choosing a dissertation topic? Try our 24/7 thesis advisory service."

To faculty in a particular discipline or department:

> "Is your research spilling over into unfamiliar territory? Let an interdisciplinary research advisory librarian help."

> "Do you know who else in the world is working in the same area as you? Ask us to check that out."

Promotion Strategy 3: Ask Users How They Heard About Your Service

In Chapter Six, "Listen to the Evaluations of Your Users" (pages 119 to 121) discusses the importance of and provides advice about soliciting evaluations from your users. For purposes of the discussion in this chapter on marketing your service, one of the proposed questions to ask on a posttransaction pop-up evaluation form—How did you hear about the service?—is especially relevant because it gives you information about the effectiveness of your marketing efforts.

Promotion Strategy 4: Keep Up with the Changing Needs in the Community

The rapid changes that are occurring in society at large are surely affecting the community you serve. So regularly take its pulse. What's new? What has changed? How do those changes affect library services?

Here are ways to keep up with the information needs of your clientele.

At least monthly, check the logs of the virtual reference questions you are getting to see whether a new area of interest or confusion is emerging. When you spot a new theme of inquiry, think about how to publicize the service to segments of your community that have the same interest. When you spot an area of confusion, think about how you can fix what caused the confusion.

When roving among users of your online tools in the library, make note of the types of questions being asked of you and periodically analyze the collective results to detect whether any new patterns of use are emerging. New patterns of use should be a signal that something significant has changed and it bears investigating in order to assess whether changes in your present service might be called for.

Once every year or two, meet in focus groups. Organize sessions with segments of your community, including current users, former users, and people who have never used the library. Try a mixture of homogeneous groups (such as parents with small children, business owners, homeless people and their social services, community leaders, recent immigrants, teenagers) and groups representing a cross section of your community. Engage the services of a professional group to conduct the meeting under your guidance but without your participation. It helps if you are present to observe the attitudes expressed in the interaction and body language, but it's important that you remain silent so that you don't inhibit frank comments.

Exercise 7–1. Conduct a survey

Conduct a survey among a sampling of your users and your nonusers. Don't ask at the outset, "Have you used our services?" or "How satisfied have you been with the service(s) you've used?" or "How can we improve?" Save those till the end. Instead ask, "Where do you go when you need information?"

Sample survey questions:

Describe the nature of the information you look for.
Where do you look for it?

Answers to these two questions will tell you whether people are going elsewhere for information they could better get from the library. With this knowledge, you can work toward tailoring your services and changing their information-seeking behaviors.

The examples in Promotion Strategy 2 (page 132) describe the same service to different segments of your clientele. Once you learn through your marketing efforts of unique needs of different segments of your community, you should design unique services directed at those special-interest groups. Because technology can help with delivering many of these unique services, it is possible for a library to come closer than ever to its goal of addressing the diverse needs of the diverse individuals in its community, so a truly responsive library will aim to design a service that satisfies an information need that is expressed by a small fraction of its community. The following examples illustrate how a public library might offer different services to different constituencies.

Services customized for environmental activists:

"Ask us about legislative updates, current events related to energy and the environment, research-in-progress, ..." (Combine it with an offer for a current-awareness service.)

Services customized for a retirement community:

"Ask us when you're looking for information about health and medicine, travel, understanding today's youth, ..." (Combine it with an offer for classes in how to find this information, and direct them to Web pages you have created specifically for this segment of your community.)

Services to parents:

"Ask us about our wealth of resources on parenting, adoption, raising twins, understanding your teenager's music, . . ." (Combine it with a referral to your Web pages containing resources devoted to these topics; hold monthly meetings, organized by parents, in which a reference librarian shows off information resources related to the theme of the meeting.)

Services to people with physical disabilities:

"Ask us about the large-print and audio resources, both in the library and via the Internet, and other services for people with physical disabilities." (Combine it with a referral to your Web pages containing relevant resources.)

When you have devised the angle of your approach to a particular group, you then position your virtual reference service to take their requests by enabling people to enter your service by the terms you used in your publicity. Some virtual library services achieve a version of this positioning by requesting that users first indicate a category in which their question falls, such as business, sports, or health. The librarian answering the call may be the specialist in that area, or, if a generalist, can know at the outset something about the context within which the user is asking the question.

Reference

Beall, Jeffrey. 1998. "Guaranteed Hits: How to Make Your Library's Web Site Stand Out in Web Search Engines." *C&RL News* (March): 160–162.

Chapter Eight
Let the Service Sell Itself

In some ways, this chapter logically follows Chapter Six on planning a user-friendly Web site in that it contains further guidelines for making your virtual reference Web site a comfortable place to visit. However, I have placed it here, following the chapter on marketing and publicizing, to tie design principles that promote a user-friendly site to those that attract new users. I hoped this sequence would emphasize the importance of the usability of your service within the context of word-of-mouth marketing. (For information about the techniques of "word-of-mouth marketing," search under that phrase in your various finding tools.)

The previous chapter covered methods of publicizing your service. If your campaign is successful, users will come to your service in droves with expectations about getting their questions answered. Of course, you hope your service will meet those expectations, because not only do you want satisfied clients, but you also know that a good service is its own publicity. Every client who has a happy experience using the service is a walking advertisement for it, and soon word-of-mouth alone will increase your business. Conversely, every client who has a frustrating experience using the service will surely tell others, to the point where people who have never tried the service could damage its reputation.

Unfortunately, in the virtual reference environment, there is a lot of frustration-making technology that users must manipulate, both before they reach you and during the reference transaction. (See Chapter Three, pages 41 to 50, for software features that can make a difference in how easy it is to use your service.) You don't want to add to the frustration by introducing confusion in areas where you have control. Luckily, there are many such areas, so there is a lot you can do to offset clients' discouraging experiences imposed by the technology. This chapter considers the characteristics of your service that you can control and provides design guidelines for counterbalancing the weak spots caused by your software. Bear in mind that your goal is to provide a *consistent* quality service, one that minimizes the likelihood of unwanted surprises, regardless of who uses the service or which staff person serves them.

Guidelines for Designing a High-Volume Service

Easy to Access

This is a must: Make your service accessible directly from the top page of your site. Do not hide your service beneath a descending hierarchy of links, such as:

Library Homepage ➡

    Library Services ➡

        Reference Services ➡

            The Librarian Is In [live, interactive service]

Make your service accessible *directly* via several paths. The more the better. For example, have a persistent link on all pages of your in-library Internet and online catalog stations; put a link on the homepages of businesses and services in your community or departments on your campus.

Obtain a URL for your service that is easy to remember. (Test the ease of remembering it with your users.) The easier it is to remember the URL, the easier it is to use it from any Internet connection without needing to rely on a bookmark. Whatever your top-level domain (.edu, .gov, etc.), get the same main domain name with a .com extension, so when only the main domain name is used and the browser automatically supplies .com, it will access your service.

Poor: www.lib.main-domain-name.edu/vrs

Poor: www.library.city.ci.us/askus

Better: askmylibrary.com

> Because this combines common words, however, it will often be misremembered (one's memory might substitute another pronoun or drop it, as in, for example, ask*thelibrary* or ask*yourlibrary*, or ask*alibrary*).

Best: *a-unique-name*.com

> QandAcafe is good, as long as it works as Q&Acafe. Using just one word, preferably a bit startling, is ideal. The word need not have anything to do with questions and answers or the library. Think of how Google and Yahoo! stick in your mind. Good ones such as Chaos and Nepenthe are taken, but you get the idea.

Easy to navigate

Create an unambiguous ambiance. Make your homepage uncomplicated by implementing the basic principles of Web homepage design in Chapter Six (pages 91 to 121). Figure 8–1 is an example of a virtual reference service homepage that is uncomplicated and makes clear how to engage the service.

Figure 8–1 Helsinki City Library's Information Gas Station chat service (http://igs.kirjastot.fi/index3.html)

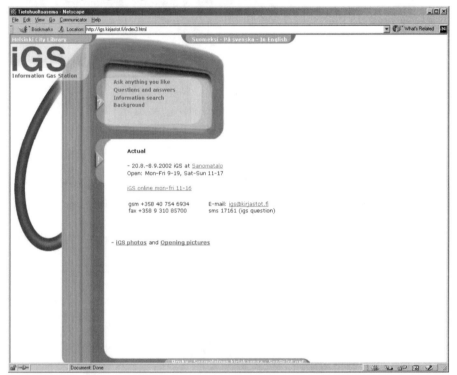

Make it easy to get back to where you were. To see how a library uses overlays to achieve this end, go to the homepage of the Toronto Public Library (www.tpl.toronto.on.ca), as shown in Figure 8–2a. Then click on one of the larger blocks along the left side of the screen or on one of the smaller blocks in the center. Figure 8–2b shows a highlighted block (lower left), with its mouse-over definition inserted in the block. When it is clicked, the corresponding page is overlaid on the homepage, slightly smaller, which makes it easy to close, bringing the user back to the homepage.

Avoid use of frames. A page with frames is harder to bookmark and can cause printing problems. Users not familiar with frames

Figure 8–2a **Homepage of the Toronto Public Library (www.tpl. toronto.on.ca)**

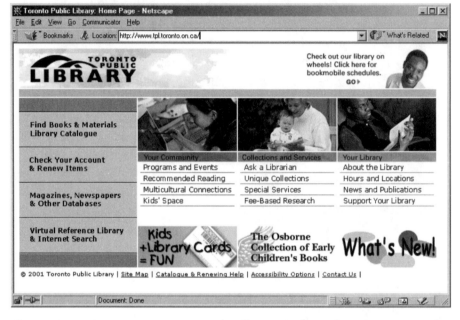

Figure 8–2b **Same homepage as in Figure 8–2a, with the lower left link highlighted (and which, when clicked, will generate an overlaid screen)**

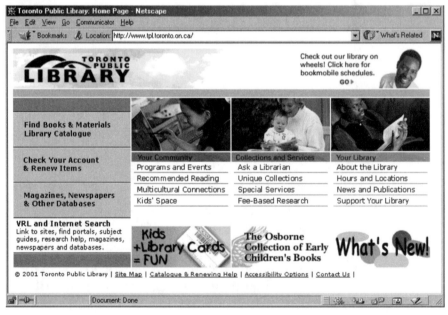

may become confused about why something they expected to happen didn't, or why something they didn't expect to happen did.

Maintain a consistent look and feel among all the main subpages of your library's Web site. Your virtual reference software is likely to provide this consistency, so this guideline applies to the rest of your site, on the premise that you want the user's entire experience with your online library to be as self-evident as possible. Your aim is to make the site's structure apparent, enabling the user to develop a conceptual navigation model of your site.

To achieve this structure, reserve parts of the screen—usually but not necessarily the perimeter—for the consistent design, and apply that design throughout your site, always making it easy to get back to your homepage. Types of information, formats, and typography of information, links, and logos that you repeat from one page to another should be positioned in the same place on each page, so that once clients use one screen of your site, they can transfer their knowledge and successfully predict where to find similar information on your other screens. The rest of the space on the screens should have unique designs. Too much sameness not only will be boring, but the viewers may assume they had already seen it and might not read or notice important parts.

Figures 8–3a through 8–3d on the next two pages are the homepages and selected subpages of one library system that provide conceptual transferability by their consistent look and feel. That is, a look at just one or two pages gives the user a sense of how to navigate the entire site. Don't try to read the tiny texts on the screens; instead, focus on the issue of a consistent look and feel.

Easy to read

Choose typography and colors that enhance readability. Use Uppercase and Lowercase Text (including for headings). ALL UPPERCASE TEXT IS HARDER TO READ.
The text color should have high contrast against the color of the background. For example, black text on a white background is easier to read than yellow on white.

Person-to-person

Speak to the user. Use personal pronouns and active verbs. Examples:
• City of Mountain View Public Library's Q&A Cafe's mission: *Our mission is to connect you with the information you need for business, work, school, home, and other needs.* See www.ci. mtnview.ca.us/citydepts/lib/fr/qanda.htm.

Figure 8–3a **Homepage of the University of Wisconsin-Madison Libraries (www.library.wisc.edu)**

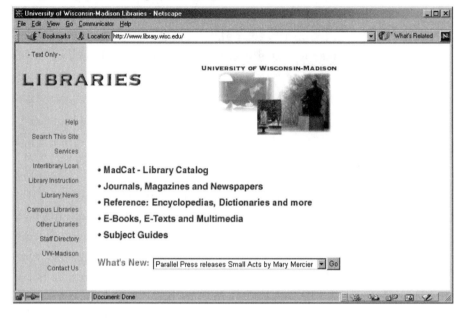

Figure 8–3b **Main page of a subsection of the University of Wisconsin-Madison Libraries' site**

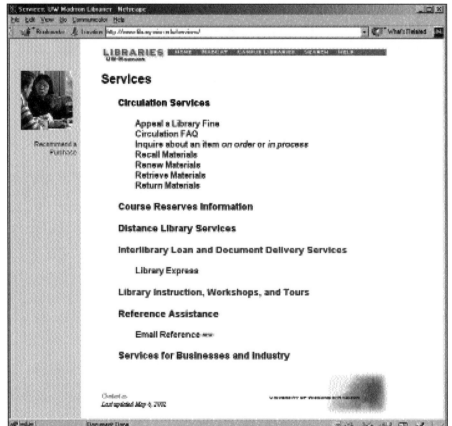

Figure 8–3c Main page of a different subsection of the University of Wisconsin-Madison Libraries' site

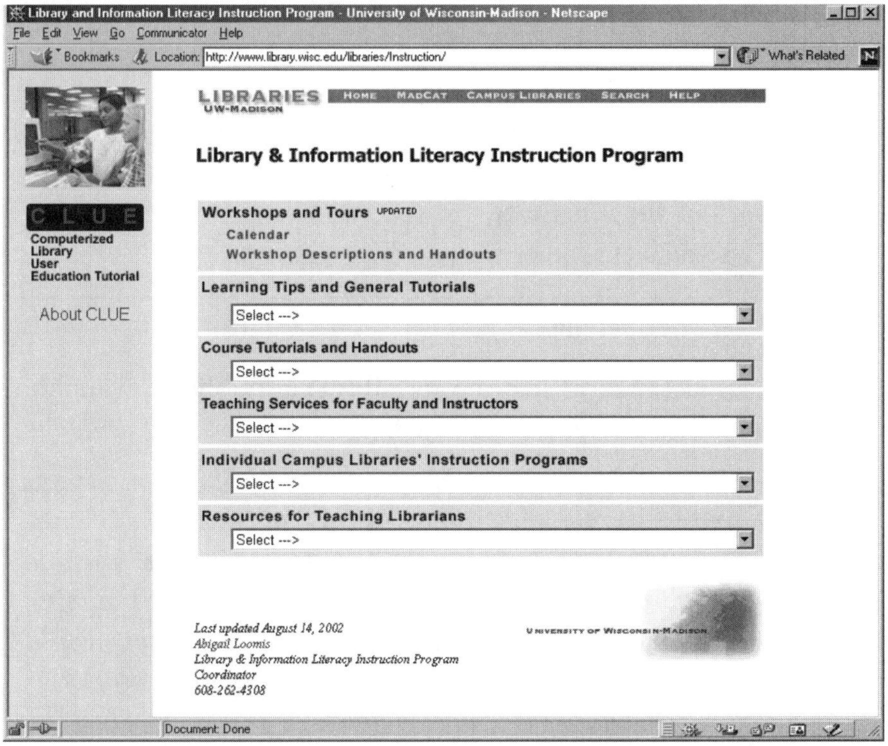

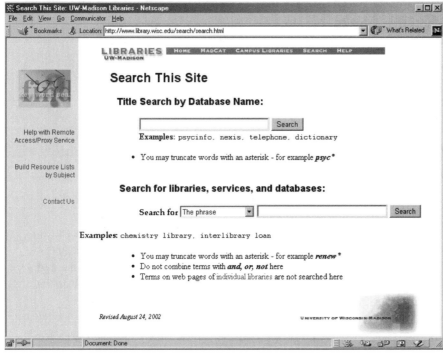

Figure 8–3d Main page of a different subsection of the University of Wisconsin-Madison Libraries' site

- Three Texas public libraries' welcome to their networked virtual reference service:

Welcome to the Answer Zone, your live online connection to library staff.

Answer Zone staff are here to help you find answers to your questions, assist you in using online resources, finding materials in the catalog or to be your tour guide when you get lost on the information superhighway.

See www.answerzone.org.

Exercise 8–1. Get personal

Here is an excerpt from one library's publicly available "online reference service policy."

Patrons may submit reference questions through email and expect an answer or a reply (if no answer can be obtained) within a 24 hour period. Acceptable questions would include requests for brief factual information or assistance with finding and using appropriate resources. Unacceptable questions would include requests for all the research necessary to do a project or research paper. This service is available 7 days a week when the library is open. It will not be available during periods when the library is closed.

How would you change it so you (a person) are speaking to the client (a person) using personal pronouns and active verbs? Also, on the principle of "the less text the better," try to cut in half the number of words without losing any part of the intended message.

Engaging

Make the user want to stay and return. Here are some ways to ensure a winning site:

- Have meaty content, and just the right amount, on each page. The user should feel that the visit to that page was worthwhile.
- Use motion sparingly. Do not overload the senses. Never have something moving rapidly and continuously. If you rotate images, as "spots" to call attention to new or special content, pause for four or five seconds before displaying the next image. For an example of a rotating centerpiece, go to the homepage of Charlotte & Mecklenburg County Library homepage (www.plcmc.lib.nc.us). (See figures 6–4a and 6–4b on page 96.)
- Use sound sparingly. It's probably best not to use background music. People's tastes vary; you're liable to turn off as many people as you please. On the

other hand, using audio for storyhour is a must, and making sound optional to accompany text can be very engaging. Be sure to provide headphones when sound is used.

- Enable interaction between the user and the function being used, such as in a how-to-use-the-online-catalog tutorial.
- Make it easy to contact a library staff member, including a particular named individual.
- Provide new news or other new content on your homepage regularly.

Frustration-free

The punch list. Once you've got the big issues under control—the site is easy to access, use, and read—check for the little things that go wrong. If uncorrected, they may not only cause frustration but could also give the impression of a sloppy, uncaring service.

- Use link-checking software to check for (and prevent) blind links.
- Avoid jargon or define it.
- Proofread for misspellings and grammatical errors.
- Identify your organization on every page, and make sure all pages have a link to your homepage. You want to help the users who bypass your homepage and jump directly to an internal page on your site to know where they are.
- Weed! Regularly monitor the pages of your site to be sure they contain current information. Delete out-of-date information.
- Test your colors with people who have different degrees of color blindness.
- Create a link to a page that explains how to change the font size to accommodate people who need a larger font.

For a thorough coverage of Web site design, see *Web Style Guide: Basic Design Principles for Creating Web Sites* by Patrick J. Lynch and Sarah Horton. New Haven: Yale University Press, 1999. Available online: www.med.yale.edu/caim/manual/contents.html.

Also see "The Alertbox: Current Issues in Web Usability," a biweekly column by Dr. Jakob Nielsen, Nielsen Norman Group. Available online: www.useit.com/alertbox/.

Usability Is in the Eye of the Beholder

Most important, let samplings of your users judge the usability of your site. Users of your service are the only yardstick you can use to measure its user-friendliness. The high marks you might give it are irrelevant if your users disagree. See the section in Chapter Six titled "Listen to the Evaluations of Your Users" (pages 119 to 121) for methods of evaluating your service and suggested questions to ask. One of the suggested questions is particularly relevant for purposes of this discussion because, being a neutral question (as described in Appendix 2, pages 157 to 160), it contains no prompting, so the impetus for the response originates entirely within the responder:

What I would really like to say about using this service is:

_____

Here's to Your Success!

If you follow the advice in this chapter, your traffic will increase, especially with repeat users. And if you heed the advice in the previous chapter on ways to promote your service, you will be busier than ever with new users. That's when to think about increasing the size of your network. Your success will also lead you to think about new services, which brings me back to the claim made in the Preface: *This book is intended as an opening argument for the imperative of developing an entire cyberbranch of your library.* But that's the subject of a different book, one I hope you will write.

Appendices
Virtual Reference Support Materials

APPENDIX 1
Causes of Questions at the Reference Desk: A Survey

Exercise A1–1. Determine the causes of questions

1. Designate a coordinator to oversee the implementation of this survey. The coordinator is responsible for the following activities:

    -   Review the categories and format of the worksheets, and revise either or both to best suit your library environment.*
    -   Choose an acceptable starting and ending date for Week 1 and Week 2.
    -   Implement Week 1 as described below.
    -   Collect and tabulate data for Week 1.
    -   Prepare Week 2 worksheets with additional categories that subsume the questions in the "Other" category of Week 1.
    -   Implement Week 2 as described below.
    -   Collect and tabulate data, and distribute results.

2. Week 1: For five consecutive weekdays and one weekend, staff keep hash-mark track of the types of questions asked at the reference desk using the worksheets (labeled "Week 1" and "Weekend 1") on the following pages. Remember, you may use the categories as listed or ones you revised or added to better reflect your library's environment.

3. Week 2: Using new charts that include additional categories that take into account the uncategorizable questions in "Other" of Week 1 and Weekend 1, keep hash-mark track of questions for an additional five consecutive weekdays and one weekend. ("Other" should still be a category.)

4. Coordinator tabulates the data by following the instructions on the tally sheet.

5. Analyze the results.

    Questions to ask yourself:

    a. No. 5, Subject advice, is the only category that is exclusively the domain of the reference professional. What percent of the total is our No. 5?

b. To what extent can the other types of questions be reduced or eliminated through better signage, changes in room arrangements, contacting the source of the problem, better instructional materials (printed and online), a clearer Web site, and so forth?

c. To what extent can the other types of questions be handled by paraprofessional staff trained in question-handling techniques (so they know what they don't know and will therefore refer the client on as needed), catalog searching methods, browser manipulation, and such?

---

* The worksheets are also on the accompanying CD-Rom. In addition to adding categories, you may change the worksheet headings to indicate individual library branches or public service units, and you may choose to tally them together or break them into separate groups. (For example, you may want to separate public service units of the general library from those devoted to special collections, since the latter's responses may distort the results.) Also, in amalgamating the tallies, you may want to keep the weekday tallies separate from the weekend tallies in order to learn whether there are discernable differences between questions asked during the week (assumed to be predominantly by your primary clientele) and those asked on the weekends, when you may have more one-time-only visitors.

CAUSES OF QUESTIONS ASKED AT THE REFERENCE DESK WEEK 1						
Category of Question	**Monday**	**Tuesday**	**Wednesday**	**Thursday**	**Friday**	**Total**
1. Directional ("Where is/are...?"; "On what floor/shelf is this call number...?")						
2. Known item request (Requests specific item by title or name; hours; phone numbers; desk reference item, etc.)						
3. Confusing class assignment (Student wants help interpreting assignment)						
4. Searched in vain on shelves (Doesn't understand shelving arrangement; items misshelved, etc.)						
5. Subject advice (Needs consultation about research topic; needs help finding information on a topic)						
6. Technology assistance (Needs help in searching a database, using a browser, etc.)						
7. Equipment/facilities (Asks about printer, copy cards, laptop connections, group study rooms, carrels, paper jams, change machines, pencil sharpeners, etc.)						
8. Other library services (Asks about ILL, circulation privileges, group instruction, etc.)						
9. Complaints						
10. Out-of-scope (So you refer to appropriate resource—e.g., "Please translate this [non-English language] paragraph"; "I'd like the name of a good lawyer"; "Can you help me fill out this tax form?")						
Other Use separate sheet to note the questions you assign here (to be categorized later)						

CAUSES OF QUESTIONS ASKED AT THE REFERENCE DESK
WEEKEND 1

Category of Question	Saturday	Sunday	Total
1. Directional ("Where is/are...?"; "On what floor/shelf is this call number...?")			
2. Known item request (Requests specific item by title or name; hours; phone numbers; desk reference item, etc.)			
3. Confusing class assignment (Student wants help interpreting assignment)			
4. Searched in vain on shelves (Doesn't understand shelving arrangement; items misshelved, etc.)			
5. Subject advice (Needs consultation about research topic; needs help finding information on a topic)			
6. Technology assistance (Needs help in searching a database, using a browser, etc.)			
7. Equipment/facilities (Asks about printer, copy cards, laptop connections, group study rooms, carrels, paper jams, change machines, pencil sharpeners, etc.)			
8. Other library services (Asks about ILL, circulation privileges, group instruction, etc.)			
9. Complaints			
10. Out-of-scope (So you refer to appropriate resource—e.g., "Please translate this [non-English language] paragraph"; "I'd like the name of a good lawyer"; "Can you help me fill out this tax form?")			
Other Use separate sheet to note the question (to be categorized later)			

CAUSES OF QUESTIONS ASKED AT THE REFERENCE DESK WEEK 2						
Category of Question	**Monday**	**Tuesday**	**Wednesday**	**Thursday**	**Friday**	**Total**
1. Directional ("Where is/are...?"; "On what floor/shelf is this call number...?")						
2. Known item request (Requests specific item by title or name; hours; phone numbers; desk reference item, etc.)						
3. Confusing class assignment (Student wants help interpreting assignment)						
4. Searched in vain on shelves (Doesn't understand shelving arrangement; items misshelved, etc.)						
5. Subject advice (Needs consultation about research topic; needs help finding information on a topic)						
6. Technology assistance (Needs help in searching a database, using a browser, etc.)						
7. Equipment/facilities (Asks about printer, copy cards, laptop connections, group study rooms, carrels, paper jams, change machines, pencil sharpeners, etc.)						
8. Other library services (Asks about ILL, circulation privileges, group instruction, etc.) 9. Complaints						
10. Out-of-scope (So you refer to appropriate resource—e.g., "Please translate this [non-English language] paragraph"; "I'd like the name of a good lawyer"; "Can you help me fill out this tax form?")						
[Add here the additional categories you created from the questions assigned to "Other" in Weekend 1]						
Other [You should end up with fewer in Week 2 than in Week 1 or Weekend 1.]						

CAUSES OF QUESTIONS ASKED AT THE REFERENCE DESK WEEKEND 2			
Category of Question	**Saturday**	**Sunday**	**Total**
1. Directional ("Where is/are…?"; "On what floor/shelf is this call number…?")			
2. Known item request (Requests specific item by title or name; hours; phone numbers; desk reference item, etc.)			
3. Confusing class assignment (Student wants help interpreting assignment)			
4. Searched in vain on shelves (Doesn't understand shelving arrangement; items misshelved, etc.)			
5. Subject advice (Needs consultation about research topic; needs help finding information on a topic)			
6. Technology assistance (Needs help in searching a database, using a browser, etc.)			
7. Equipment/facilities (Asks about printer, copy cards, laptop connections, group study rooms, carrels, paper jams, change machines, pencil sharpeners, etc.)			
8. Other library services (Asks about ILL, circulation privileges, group instruction, etc.)			
9. Complaints			
10. Out-of-scope (So you refer to appropriate resource—e.g., "Please translate this [non-English language] paragraph"; "I'd like the name of a good lawyer"; "Can you help me fill out this tax form?")			
[Add here the additional categories you created from the questions assigned to "Other" in Weekend 1]			
Other [You should end up with fewer in Weekend 2 than in Weekend 1.]			

CAUSES OF QUESTIONS
ASKED AT THE REFERENCE DESK

TALLY of Weeks 1 and 2 (including Weekends)

Category of Question	A Week 1 Total	B Week 2 Total	C Weeks 1 & 2 Total	D Percent of Grand Total
1. Directional				
2. Known item request				
3. Confusing class assignment				
4. Searched in vain on shelves				
5. Subject advice				
6. Technology assistance				
7. Equipment/ facilities				
8. Other library services				
9. Complaints				
10. Out-of-scope				
[Add here the additional categories you created for Week 2]				
Other				
GRAND TOTAL (Add Column C)				100%

APPENDIX 2
Neutral Questioning: Why It Works, What It Looks Like, and How to Modify It for the Virtual Environment

Tip: Avoid starting your question with an auxiliary verb
Closed questions start with one of he following verbs:
is, an, are, was, were, have, has, had, do, does, did, may, can, must, might, could, would, should, shall, will

In Part 1, Chapter Two, Axiom 1 (page 21) is a discussion of the importance of using a method—in particular, neutral questioning (NQ)—for ensuring that you provide the client with information relevant to the request. Chapter 4 contains exercises that give you practice in neutral questioning (pages 63 to 64). For readers who are unfamiliar with the technique or who need a reminder, here are some highlights of its characteristics, as well as examples of neutral questions. Also included is the adjustment to the technique to suit the virtual environment.

Required Characteristics of a Neutral Question

- A neutral question can never be a "closed question," that is, one that has a limited number of responses, such as one that can be answered by yes or no, or one that asks to choose from alternatives you provide ("Do you want the information to be recent? Historical? Comprehensive? An overview?")
  Explanation: Closed questions lead the client down a road you've already chosen, a path you don't want to take as a first response.

- A neutral question is a type of "open question," one to which the client responds with information that is directly relevant to his or her situation.
  Explanation: An "open question" that is not a neutral question may encourage the client to freely talk about things that are not related to the situation. By asking a neutral question, you don't waste time dealing with irrelevant information.

- A neutral question includes no noun, adjective, or adverb used in the client's question.
  Explanation: To get at the client's "real" question efficiently, you need to prevent yourself from making assumptions based on the client's opening question. Eliminating the client's nouns, adjectives, or adverbs keeps you from expressing your assumptions.

For example: The client asks for material on large cities in China. Your response must not include "large" or "cities" or "China" on the premise that the client's "real" question may have nothing to do with cities or even China, and if it did, "large" may not be the appropriate term for the size of cities wanted. So, a bad response would be "What do you mean by large?" Whereas a good response would be "Tell me more about what you're hoping to find."

- A neutral question does not begin with "Why."
  Explanation: "Why" questions put the client on the defensive, as if you are requiring the client to justify asking the question at all.

- A neutral question gives the client control over the direction you take to fulfill the request.
  Explanation: By being free of assumptions, your neutral question will enable the client to restate the problem, so that you may proceed to search for information relevant to that restated problem.

The Technique of a Neutral Question

For subject questions (e.g., "Can you help me find material on subject x?"), in the face-to-face environment you should respond directly with a neutral question. When the question is for a specific resource or fact, you will usually need to give the client a reason for answering your neutral question, even if you expect the answer will be a repeat of the question originally asked. Because you have only a few seconds to hold a client's attention, that reason should be the first words out of your mouth. For example:

- The client is asking for a specific resource, such as a nonfiction book title.
  Opener: I'll be happy to check for you, and we have other/more current/more comprehensive materials on the same topic as covered in that book.
  . . . followed by a neutral question, such as "Can you tell me more about what you are hoping to find?"

- The client is asking for a fact (the words to the song "Shrimp Boats Are A-comin'") or a specific topic (a biography of Upton Sinclair).
  Opener: I can look for that in several places, depending on your particular situation.
  . . . followed by a neutral question, such as "I may be able to save you time if I knew a little more" or "Is there something in particular you are expecting to do with the information?"

Modify the Technique for the Virtual Environment

At the virtual reference desk, you can talk to the client in scripted messages while conducting a search; therefore, it is usually appropriate for you to provide the client with a quick tentative answer and simultaneously ask a neutral question. In particular, when you know of an easily accessible Internet resource that will answer the question you think was asked, retrieve that resource and display it in the client's browser, and at the same time ask a neutral question, beginning with an opener (preferably one that is scripted for this circumstance).

For example:

Opener: If I understand your question, here is a document that provides some information. I can vary the search in several ways, depending on your situation.

. . . followed by a neutral question, such as "Can you say more about what you are hoping to find?"

Examples of Neutral Questions

As you gain experience using neutral questioning in different situations, you will develop a sense of when to ask a neutral question that elicits how the client intends to use the information you supply versus when to ask one that gets at what made them ask the question in the first place.

Below are sample questions, grouped into these two categories. When doing the exercises in Chapter Four (pages 65 to 68), you may create your own neutral question(s) or choose from the lists below.

Caution: Each of these questions works well for the person who contributed it, but may not work for you because of the differences in your voice, inflection, sincerity about the question's message, or a host of other reasons. So be sure to pick one(s) that you feel comfortable saying.

NQs that get at the client's goal

1. Can you describe the kind of information you would like to find?
2. Is there a specific question you are trying to answer?
3. What will this information help you do?
4. Perhaps if you could tell me what this information will help you do, I'd have a better idea of how to help you.
5. Could you tell me a bit more about what you're looking for?
6. What kind of question are you trying to answer?
7. Where would you like to go with the information?
8. What aspect of this situation concerns you?
9. Can you tell me something about how you will be using this information?
10. What are you trying to do in this situation?

11. What are you hoping to find?
12. How will this information be helpful to you?
13. What kind of help are you looking for?
14. Tell me what you're ultimately trying to do, so I can head you in the right direction.
15. Keep talking! I'm beginning to get a picture of what you are trying to do.

NQs that get at the situation that gave rise to the client's opening question

1. What can you tell me about your situation?
2. What happened that brought you to this point?
3. What's the situation you're dealing with?
4. Can you give me a little background on your interest in this?
5. What have you done so far?

APPENDIX 3
Virtual Reference Desk Service Policies, Scripted Messages, and Tales from the Trenches

Virtual reference service isn't old enough to have settled service policies in place. Libraries are either writing them from scratch or amending existing policies. Either way, they are constantly revising these policies as they learn how virtual reference service is different from service at a physical desk. The following are excerpts from several networked libraries' virtual reference service policies and guidelines. They represent the libraries' thinking of the moment and should be considered drafts that probably have undergone changes. Wherever possible, I have supplied the policy's URL so that you may check out the full and latest version, a worthwhile effort I highly recommend.

In addition to the policies of networked services represented in these excerpts, you can view the virtual reference service policies of two individual libraries online. These, too, should be regarded as works in progress.

- **University of Illinois at Urbana-Champaign**
  www.library.uiuc.edu/ugl/_staff/vr/proc.html
- **Penn State University Libraries**
  www.de2.psu.edu/faculty/saw4/vrs/ (click on *Rules* and *Privacy*)

Sample Policies and Guidelines

From the guidelines of Ready for Reference/Alliance Library System

The full and updated document is at www.alliancelibrarysystem.com/Projects/ReadyRef/Guidelines.doc.

Thanks to Alliance Library System for permission to reprint these excerpts.

Clientele served

1. Priority for service is extended to the students, faculty, staff, and others associated with the academic communities served by the eight participating libraries.

2. Next priority is given to clients within the broader communities served by the participating libraries, Illinois residents living in the 14,000-square-mile region covered by the Alliance Library System (when this can be ascertained), and Illinois residents at large.

Length of reference transactions

1. This service will handle all types of reference questions, from ready reference to those that are more in depth.
2. Ready reference questions may be answered in fewer than ten minutes.
3. In-depth reference assistance may be provided if appropriate. If a question is in depth, the provider should do his or her best to locate some sources, and offer to e-mail additional materials. With such questions, the reference provider may need to refer the client to his or her library, or to conference a librarian from the client's library in on the session. If this isn't possible, the transcript may be referred to the library's project liaison at the session's conclusion for follow-up.
4. "I will get back to you within x hours or minutes" may be used when a reference provider is close to the answer and prefers to see the question through to completion, but must check printed sources, or has others waiting for assistance.
5. Reference providers should keep their side of the dialogue brief and use message scripts whenever possible. This will help minimize the length of the session.

Responses to clients—general information

1. Generalized scripts are developed and approved by the advisory committee. This will help participants provide consistent service among libraries.
2. Reference providers, depending on their specialties, may develop personalized scripts.
3. Reference providers may use their first names and institutions, e.g., "Hello. I am Lori from Spoon River College. How may I help you?" Login and screen name changes are requested through the project director.
4. Addition of URLs to the scripted messages are based on recommendations from the reference providers and committee members.

5. Slide shows and instruction screens may be developed and uploaded for all reference providers to use.

6. Etiquette:

   a. Reference providers should expect the same etiquette from clients as they would in face-to-face interactions. Clients are expected to be polite. Do's and don'ts for clients are listed on the "chat" Web page for users' perusal.

   b. Inappropriate behavior is not to be tolerated. Providers may send the scripted warning message to the client or terminate the call. As with traditional reference service, such behavior is handled at the discretion of the reference provider. If the client becomes a perennial problem, the other reference providers should be alerted via the *readyforreference* mailing list.

Resources to be used for answering questions

It is imperative that users receive consistent service among reference service providers. It is also important to keep within the copyright and licensing restrictions at all times.

1. Online Resources:

   Tools that the participating libraries may use include the Illinois State Library–provided FirstSearch databases, the IDAL databases, and free Internet resources. Other databases may be used at the discretion of the individual librarian, who may choose to send citations of items obtainable through interlibrary loan at the client's library.

2. Sites to Avoid:

   A listing of Web sites to avoid, either due to unreliable content or "browser blowup" will be maintained at the *Ready for Reference* Web site. If a reference provider comes across such a site, he or she is asked to inform the other providers immediately through the *readyforreference* mailing list. The site will then be added to the Web-based list.

From the policies of QandAcafe during its pilot phase

Thanks to BALIS/PLS/SVLS Reference Center for permission to reprint these excerpts.

Average length of transaction

The average length of a transaction should be in the range of 7–10 minutes. This is by no means a hard-and-fast rule. However, we find that customers tend to get impatient if they are kept online much longer than that. Librarians must use their own judgment in this area. If there is nobody in the queue waiting and the patron is willing to stay online, the transaction may go longer. If the librarian is unable to answer the question in the allotted time and the patron wants the request to be continued, these procedures should be followed:

1. Follow up with the patron by phone or email . . . [details omitted].

2. Refer the question to second level reference . . . [details omitted].

3. If the question is easily answered with the print collection at the library and requires the customer to browse, search multiple copies of periodicals, or other print material, the customer will be referred to the library.

Confidentiality

In the initial stages of our pilot project, transcripts from sessions will be saved and possibly used for FAQs. Customers will be asked before logging on to the VRD whether they are willing to accept the possibility of having their transcripts retained and used in a limited way. At this point in the project, customer consent to this limited use of transactions is a requirement for service. All retained transcripts will be kept on a secure server, and no one but staff and librarians will have access to them. This policy will be reviewed at the conclusion of the pilot.

System-wide message scripts

While there will be common scripts loaded on to each login, the use of these messages will not be required. However, it is recommended that we use them as needed to uphold our standard of service with respect to both speed and courtesy. It is especially important to send quick messages to keep the customer informed about searching progress. Scripted responses are very useful for this purpose.

Scheduling and staffing

Our initial pilot project will be staffed with three librarians at all times. We will be open for the hours of 3:00 to 9:00 P.M. Monday through Friday. To begin with, each library will be required to cover four hours during these times. These hours are not necessarily consecutive and may use one to four different librarians. As we get a sense of customer demand, these times may be revised.

Service tips to ensure client satisfaction

Providing quality customer service via real-time interaction over the Internet is remarkably similar to providing quality customer service via interaction in person or over the telephone. In all three real-time modes, it is important to be professional without being overly formal or impersonal, while being friendly without being overly informal or chatty. As friendly professionals, we strive to

- Treat each customer individually.
- Get straight to the point, but do an effective reference interview to be sure you GET the question.
- Keep sentences brief.
- Let the customer know what you plan to do.
- Avoid one-word responses, since these feel terse in written exchanges.

From the policies of 24/7 Reference

The full and current document is at www.247ref.org/manual/247 policies.pdf.

Thanks to Susan McGlamery for permission to reprint these excerpts.

General guidelines

The first choice for information should be online databases or Web sites. Data entry or copy and paste into the chat box should be limited.

- Materials may be sent by fax or e-mail in response to a question received via e-mail.
- Authoritative medical, legal, and consumer report information pages may be pushed to patrons, but librarians must make it clear that the Library does not verify the accuracy of the information. The caveat about the accuracy of Web sites applies to all Web sites the librarian suggests.
- Always cite the source of the information pushed to the patron if the source is not readily apparent on the online database or Web page.
- Try to keep responses quick and factual. Do not "chat" too much with the patron. 24/7 Reference is not a chat room for lonely people. If it becomes necessary to disconnect a patron, do it politely.
- Queries that require instruction (e.g., how to use a search engine to locate information or how to use the Library online catalog) are exceptions to the quick-and-factual guideline. 24/7 Reference provides an excellent vehicle for such instruction.

  Librarians may also make virtual appointments with patrons to continue the instruction during the librarian's shift, or, in the case of librarians from member libraries, in their off-desk time.

However, 24/7 Reference does not provide extended instructional services for patrons, nor does it provide research services for patrons.

[For more of this guideline, go to the Web page cited above.]

Performance standards

Calls should be answered as quickly as possible. Try to keep sessions to 15 minutes or less. Follow the guidelines below to help keep your sessions "quick." While it is not always possible, the goal is to keep patrons waiting no more than two minutes.

Professional Service: Quality. As professional librarians, we provide quality information that meets certain criteria. Follow these guidelines to ensure a high quality response:

1. Whenever possible, use information from library resources (including the Librarians' Index to the Internet . . . or proprietary databases) to answer questions, rather than using Google or Yahoo! . . . .

2. Always use a reference source to locate the answer to a question and always give the caller the name of the source.

3. Be sure the Web sites you send match the five criteria for

   ➤ Accuracy
   ➤ Authority
   ➤ Objectivity
   ➤ Currency
   ➤ Coverage

4. If you are unable to locate an authoritative answer to a question in a timely fashion, then either get back to the patron in a few hours (do a follow-up) or refer the question to MCLS or subject expert.

From the policies of the Answer Zone

For the current version, go to www.answerzone.org/privacy.html.

Privacy policy (accessible by the public)

The Answer Zone and its participating libraries acknowledge that online security and privacy are important concerns to many of our users. No information gathered by the Answer Zone is ever given to third parties.

When logging in to the Answer Zone, you may be asked to provide your name, e-mail address, city of residence, and whether you have a library card. Not all of this data is required for our service to function, but we are better able to serve you if you do provide it. You have the option of being an anonymous user.

By providing your e-mail address you will receive a transcript of your transaction, including links to any Internet sites visited. This transcript is also sent to the staff member who assisted you, so that if you call back with a question, they are able to locate more information after your session has ended. The staff person may need to refer your question to a subject expert by forwarding the transcript to that person. Lastly, transcripts may be reviewed by supervisory staff to insure the quality of the service provided. Your e-mail address will not be used for any other purpose.

At the end of your session we ask you to complete an evaluation about the Answer Zone. The evaluation form does not collect any personal information.

Some information is logged when you access our site, but that information is for statistical purposes only, and does not lead us, or anyone else, back to you. It is data about your browser (Netscape Navigator, Internet Explorer, etc.), which operating system you use (Macintosh or Windows), and, in some cases, your Internet service provider's domain name (such as "aol.com")—not any personally identifiable information about you or your system's configuration.

The Answer Zone collects IP addresses for the purposes of system administration and for authentication.

The Answer Zone will send cookies to your computer for the purpose of accessing your previous user sessions as this may assist the staff member who helps you if you refer to a previous visit. Cookies are also used to maintain the connection between your computer and ours. We cannot and do not use them to obtain any personal data about you.

In the course of your transaction, the Answer Zone staff may send you to other sites on the Internet. You should make yourself aware of the Privacy Policies and Data Collections practices of these sites. The Answer Zone takes no responsibility or liability for the privacy policies or practices of other Internet sites.

Scripted Messages

From the QandAcafe

Thanks to BALIS/PLS/SVLS Reference Center for permission to reproduce these scripted messages.

[—INSERT(Cust.User)—], welcome to your QandAcafe reference session.

Welcome to the QandAcafe. Unfortunately, our initial rollout does not include your city. Be on the lookout. It will be coming your way soon!

If at any time a Web page blocks your chat area, just click on the back button on your browser twice.

I have your email address as [—INSERT(Cust.Mail)—], is that correct?

I have your phone number as [—INSERT(Cust.Phone)—], is that correct?

That's a good question. Let's see what we can find on that. . . .

Please hold while I see what I can find. . . .

Just a moment, please.

I'm just searching the Web, I'll get back to you with the results shortly.

I'm still looking. . . . I'll be back with you momentarily. . . .

The Web page I'll send to your screen is the Librarians' Index to the Internet. It's a reliable and efficient subject guide to Web sites. I recommend bookmarking it from the transcript at the end of the session.

I am sending you a search result. Please note, some of these links may not be current, nor hold conclusive authority. Scroll down to see all of them.

I have found something. Is it OK if I send you a page now?

Soon you'll see a Web page on your screen that I'm sending to you.

The Internet is vast and uncontrolled. The validity of any information found on the Web must be questioned as it has not been scrutinized by librarians like the resources found in the library.

Please scroll down the page using the scroll bars on the right side of the window.

Go ahead and search this site while I check out another one.

This could take a while. Would you like me to call or e-mail you when I find the information?

If you'd like, I can call and assist you simultaneously over the phone.

I think I can answer your question with a resource that is in the library. Can I get back to you with an answer?

I apologize for the delay. Our connection was broken and I've just rejoined. Do you have time for us to continue?

I haven't heard from you in a while. Are you still on the line?

Please tell me more.

What else can you tell me?

What kind of information are you looking for?

Would you explain that in more detail?

Could you be more specific about what you're looking for?

Can you tell me more about how you will be using this information?

Is that exactly what you are looking for?

Do you think this will be enough to get you started?

Does that completely answer your question?

Thank you for using the QandAcafe. If you need further help, please feel free to login again. It's been a pleasure serving you.

Due to the high call volume, sometimes it may become necessary to limit the number of questions per caller. This policy will be implemented as needed. Thank you for using our service.

Reference librarians are here to answer questions and to make referrals to other sources of information. We cannot give advice.

We have to end our session now. I hope this information was useful to you.

Tales From the Trenches

Thanks to Bernie Sloan for permission to reprint his invaluable "case studies" webliography, with a few references to articles that are not on the Web, which he posted to the livereference forum April 5, 2002 and keeps up to date at www.lis.uiuc.edu/~b-sloan/digicase.htm. *They are the stories about the thinking and the nitty-gritty that it took to launch a new service, by the people who helped to build it.*

Boyer, Joshua. "Virtual Reference at the NCSU Libraries: The First One Hundred Days." *Information Technology & Libraries* 20(3), 122–128. September 2001. www.lita.org/ital/2003_boyer.html.

Broughton, Kelly. "Our Experiment in Online, Real-time Reference." *Computers in Libraries* 21(4), 26–31. April 2001. www.infotoday.com/cilmag/apr01/broughton.htm.

Cichanowicz, Edana McCaffery. "Sunday Night Live! An Experiment in Live Reference Chat." *NyLink Connection* 3(1), 8–9. Spring 2001. http://nylink.suny.edu/docu/nc/NCspr01.pdf (Link is to entire issue; see page 8)

Cichanowicz, Edana M. "Sunday Night Live! An Experiment in Real-time Reference Chat—on a Shoestring Budget." *The Charleston Advisor* 2(4) 49–51. April 15, 2001. www.charlestonco.com/features.cfm?id=59&type=fr

Fagan, Judy Condit, and Michele Calloway. "Creating an Instant Messaging Reference System." *Information Technology & Libraries* 20(4), 202–212. December 2001. www.lita.org/ita/2004_fagan.html

Foley, Marianne. "Instant Messaging Reference in an Academic Library: A Case Study." *College and Research Libraries* 63(1), 36–45. January 2002.

Heilig, Jean M. "Virtual Reference at Jones University." *Colorado Libraries* 27(2), 35–37. Summer 2001.

Hoag, Tara J., and Edana McCaffery Cichanowicz. "Going Prime Time with Live Chat Reference." *Computers in Libraries* 21(8), 40–45. September 2001.

Holmer, Susan E., and Janie B. Silveria. "Food for Thought at the QandAcafé." Information Strategies 2001, Holiday Inn Select, Fort Myers, Florida, November 14–16, 2001. http://library.fgcu.edu/Conferences/ infostrategies/ presentations/2001/holmer.htm

Kawakami, Alice K. "Delivering Digital Reference." NetConnect Supplement to *Library Journal*, 28–29. Spring 2002. http://libraryjournal. reviewsnews. com/index.asp?layout=articleid=CA210717

Kibbee, Jo, David Ward, and Wei Ma. "Virtual Reference, Real Data: Results of a Pilot Study." *Reference Services Review* 30(1), 25–36. 2002.

Lindbloom, Mary-Carol. "Ready for Reference: Academic Libraries Offer Live Web-based Reference." Final Narrative Report (an LSTA-funded project). www.alliancelibrarysystem.com/projects/readyref/FinalReport.doc

Marsteller, Matt, and Paul Neuhaus. "The Chat Reference Experience at Carnegie Mellon University." Presentation at American Library Association Annual Conference, 2001. www.contrib.andrew.cmu.edu/~matthewm/ALA_2001_chat.html

Mathews, Brian, et al. "Real-time Reference Round-up." Information Strategies 2001, Holiday Inn Select, Fort Myers, Florida, November 14–16, 2001. http://library.fgcu.edu/Conferences/infostrategies/presentations/2001/viggiano.htm

Sears, JoAnn. "Chat Reference Service: An Analysis of One Semester's Data." *Issues in Science & Technology Librarianship* 32, Fall 2001. www.istl.org/istl/01-fall/article2.html

Sloan, Bernie. "Ready for Reference: Academic Libraries Offer Live Web-Based Reference." Evaluating System Use. Final Report. July 11, 2001. www.lis. uiuc. edu/~b-sloan/r4r.final.htm

Sloan, Bernie. "Reference Service in the Digital Library: A Report on the Ready for Reference Project." *Library Hi Tech News* 18(10). December 2001.

Stormont, Sam. "Interactive Reference Project: Assessment After Two Years." Paper presented at Facets of Digital Reference Service: The Virtual Reference Desk Second Annual Digital Reference Conference, October 16–17, 2000. www.vdr.org/conferences/VRD2000/proceedings/stormont.shtml

APPENDIX 4
Chat Communication Tips

Jana Ronan's Chat Communication Tips

A document of the University of Florida Libraries' RefeXpress service, Jana Ronan's Chat Communication Tips are presented here (with minor editing) with her permission. See updates at www.uflib.ufl.edu/hss/ref/rxchat.html.

- Talk in short sentences. Lengthy paragraphs of text take a long time to type and are hard to read in a chat window.
- If you need to communicate in a lengthy sentence or paragraph, break it up into chunks.
- Give the client lots of feedback. The danger of not giving enough feedback is that clients may feel ignored or that they have been disconnected.
- If you type slowly, tell the client.
- If you have a slow connection, let the client know.
- If the question is a tough one, tell the client that it's going to take a while to answer the question.
- Remember that clients can't see or hear you. Tell them what you are doing. If you are going to consult a book or go to the stacks, don't forget to tell the client.
- What's the client's time frame? Offer to e-mail answers if the client is in a hurry.
- Conduct a reference interview and determine whether the client needs an immediate answer or would like to learn how to find the information.
- Expect transactions to take longer than those at the reference desk.
- Keep the client engaged in the process to find an answer. If you estimate that it is going to take some time, give the client something to do. Here are some suggestions:

  ✓ Have the client search the database too (if appropriate).
  ✓ When finding an answer involves searching more than one database, set up the client to search in one while you search in another.
  ✓ Offer to e-mail the answer if the answer lends itself to an e-mail.
  ✓ Ask the client a question every now and then.
  ✓ Describe what you are finding as you go along.
  ✓ Ask what the client is finding (if the client is searching too).
  ✓ If the client will be left waiting a while, use a "hold" script. This is a NetAgent feature that keeps the client informed that the connection is indeed still alive and you are working on the question. It can be pro-

grammed to deliver different messages automatically at time intervals you specify. For example, the client might see: "I'm still working on your question. Be right back." Then, 30 seconds later, "Don't go away. I almost have the answer."

24/7 Reference Chat Tips (excerpts)

For the full and current document, go to www.247ref.org/manual/reference_tips.cfm.

Thanks to Susan McGlamery for permission to reproduce these tips.

Reference

Our goal is to answer questions as quickly as possible. Try not to stay online with anyone for longer than 15 or 20 minutes, less time if possible.

Keep sending brief chat messages every 30–45 seconds or so.

If you can't find anything in 15–20 minutes, send the Follow-Up chat message. . . .

Sometimes, when searching library catalogs for audiobooks, the limit option may leave out some relevant titles. If this happens, try leaving out the limit by format and add a keyword or title keyword search for sound recording.

If you have a question you think you might have to transfer out, it might be a good idea to spend more time conducting the reference interview, because the information will help MCLS's second-level reference.

If the patron disconnects before the answer is given, continue the conversation and give the patron the answer if it is possible and no one is waiting. The patron will receive the transcript of the session via e-mail anyway, so it will save the time of having to send another e-mail.

It might be useful to ask a patron, "What type of information have you looked at so far, so I don't duplicate your search?"

It might be appropriate to say sometimes when there is a patron waiting, "Do you need any more help from me?" or "May I go help another person?"

If a patron seems like a kid who needs articles for a research report, it's useful to ask the grade level. EBSCOHost's PrimarySearch database gives reading levels to help distinguish articles that are for certain grade levels.

If you get a question that could best be answered by a database search, or if someone has a question about a database and you do not feel that you can answer it effectively (because of your access problems), please transfer the request to the MCLS Ref waiting room, which we at MCLS will be monitoring.

If, when picking up a patron, it shows that the patron has disconnected, but you can still read the question and the e-mail address, send an e-mail to the patron with the answer, if possible, or ask for more information. That way we can minimize "dropped calls" and provide the best possible service.

Check spelling when sending chat. Make sure to use the proper forms of its, it's, your, you're, there, their, and other troublesome words.

Look at the patron's e-mail address to see whether it looks reasonable. For example, make sure it has an @ sign, and make sure there are no obvious typos, such as exite.com instead of excite.com. If there are typos or it looks like the the e-mail address is invalid, then ask the patron if the address is correct. If there is no @ sign, ask the patron if their Internet service is AOL. If the e-mail address is invalid or incorrect, the transcript will not be sent to the patron. If you are able to ascertain the correct e-mail address, then once the transcript has arrived in the archive, forward a copy to the patron's correct e-mail address. The transcript may appear in the "Test" folder in the archive since there was no valid e-mail address.

Special libraries can be great places to refer patrons to if they need several specialized sources. Special libraries may or may not be open to the public, though, so it might be a good idea to mention that when making a referral. Here's a site that offers links to Southern California special libraries. It is updated frequently: http://home.earthlink.net/~jsmog/library3.html.

APPENDIX 5
Training for Change: Beyond the Virtual Reference Desk

That the content that follows has been relegated to an appendix is not to be taken as a sign that it is unimportant. On the contrary, from my standpoint, in a broader book about change in libraries that included virtual reference service, this would be a leading section. However, it is "extra" in that it covers ideas that are tangential to the subject of this book, virtual reference service, and I didn't want to risk your stumbling over (or never getting to) ideas about virtual reference because you were stuck arguing with some of the larger issues that are discussed here.

Note: Parts of this appendix were originally written for an article to appear in *Internet Reference Services Quarterly*, titled "The Librarian Has Left the Building, but Whereto?" (Lipow, 2003).

This book is about virtual reference, how to prepare for it, train for it, and make it a busy service. But if libraries stop there, they will be doing nothing more than taking advantage of a new technology to provide the same service, just as they have always done. They will be closing their eyes and ears to opportunities that would move libraries to a new level of networking and establish a new definition for the professional work of librarians. If we are to be taken seriously as professional workers, we must be far more involved than we have been in the re-engineering of our services and far more analytical about the reference librarian's role in answering questions.

Our myopia serves to limit our use of new technologies to help maintain the status quo. "Same old service, brand-new technology," explained a manager of a busy 24/7 networked virtual reference service in a talk to a large audience of librarians who had recently launched or were about to embark on such a service. She was probably trying to allay their fears about the unknowns of such a major change. However, in doing so, she inadvertently closed the door to new concepts and opportunities that would be the prerequisites for making fundamental and necessary changes in our profession.

Her words reminded me of what we librarians said decades ago to our users who regarded the newfangled online public catalog with great trepidation. "Not to worry," we reassured them. "This catalog is just like your old friend the card catalog . . . ." The trouble with that comparison was that it encouraged users to maintain the same mental model of the online catalog as they held of the card catalog, whose searchability was based on very limited concepts. Also, such a comparison increased the likelihood that users' misconceptions about the card catalog (and they had many!) would be carried over to the online catalog, where they would continue search habits that should have long before been broken. This limited vision is even carried over to the homepages of some libraries' Web sites, where there are links to the "Online Card Catalog."

Indeed, when a change seems to threaten the status quo, it may be rejected outright. As applied to virtual reference, for example, one academic librarian reports her observation that many students with questions don't ask them at the reference desk because they don't want to "face the humiliation of being seen asking for help in public." However, she concludes that virtual reference is inferior to face-to-face reference because it lacks the information-packed visual cues present in the physical environment, and the virtual staff person, who could be anywhere on the globe, has no knowledge of the context of the student's question. (Fister, 2002) This reasoning discounts a plethora of contrary evidence: testimony from countless users of both e-mail and chat reference services that say they appreciate the anonymity and find it easier (perhaps less "humiliating"?) to express what they really want. It also ignores the experience of networked librarians who, because they can review one another's work, keep improving their service to the "other's" clients.

One reason a limited vision is so prevalent in our profession is that the library work environment discourages creative thinking. If we change that environment, we will move faster beyond the "horseless carriage" analogy to virtual reference that Clifford Lynch talks of in the Foreword.

In the hopes of encouraging discussions about how to achieve an environment in which staff is valued for its creative ideas, problem-solving contributions, and openness to new ways of working, I have drawn a verbal sketch of what I consider to be the ideal but feasible components of a library that keeps up in fast-changing times.

Ideal Component 1: A Climate of Learning

A no-blame environment

Until you can prove otherwise, assume staff members who made a mistake or showed poor judgment were doing their best under the particular circumstances. A supervisor might underscore this attitude by letting the staff know, and showing, that in the interests of continuous improvement, their willingness and efforts to identify problems is most appreciated, and, if they can suggest solutions, all the better. With this positive attitude prevailing,

a. a staff member who makes a mistake or shows faulty judgment is willing to talk about it, knowing that the response will be: "We know you were doing the best you could at the time. Let's figure out how to avoid this in the future."

b. a staff member can raise a problem seemingly caused by another employee's work, knowing that the other employee will not be punished but instead will be trusted to have done the best that person could do at the time and would be included in discussions about how to avoid the problem. Working in this milieu, there's a good chance the source of the problem lies either in an undertrained staff person or in somewhere other than a particular employee's faulty work.

c. a staff member who suggests a new way of doing things has support in testing that new way and isn't penalized if the idea doesn't work out.

d. "Resisters" are listened to with a positive ear:

- A staff member who rejects someone else's new idea is not labeled "out of touch"; instead, the knee-jerk assumption is that the promoter of the idea hasn't explained it or proven its merits well enough.
- The staff person who says "I'm too old to learn" or "I won't be able to do that; I have no head for technology" or "Just let me be till I retire in four years" should be heard as saying either "I worry that after being competent for so many years, I'll become incompetent" or "I'd be willing to try it if I'm given adequate time to learn."

A staff with up-to-date skills and knowledge

In a fast-changing environment, a programmatic approach to staff development is critical for maintaining staff competencies. Two measures of this approach are as follows:

a. A continuous education program is evident. In areas where the new knowledge, skill, procedure, or other new way of thinking and operating is essential, attendance at training programs is required.

b. Skills or knowledge that should be candidates for staff training are those required of newly hired staff but that the current staff doesn't possess

A challenged staff

The library fosters curiosity and love of learning by holding regular meetings in which staff can discuss issues in flux, challenge long-held beliefs, and raise thought-provoking questions for which there are no clear answers, such as:

- **Do our clients really understand our terminology?**
- **How do licensing agreements, copyright law, and fair use guidelines apply to pushing pages to clients of a virtual reference service?**
- **As e-book technology improves and e-books become more prevalent, what is likely to be the impact on libraries?**
- **How can we reconcile our promise to clients of maintaining confidentiality and our desire to give them individual service?**
- **How can we square our commitment to open access to information and our desire to protect children from the hard-to-define category of "objectionable material"?**
- **What difference does the MLS make?**

A *eu*stressed staff

Just as there is a bad cholesterol and a good cholesterol, there is a bad kind of stress and a good kind of stress. A *dis*tressed staff, one that feels it has neither control over its work nor influence on the changes being imposed, is the kind to prevent or minimize. A *eu*stressed staff (*eu-* being a prefix meaning "good," as in *eulogy* and *euphoria*) is one to strive for. Characteristics of a eustressed person are the following:

- **comfortable not knowing it all**
- **optimistic**
- **reacts openly to new ideas**
- **self-confident, undefensive**
- **curious, loves learning, stretching the mind, growing**
- **has a high "emotional intelligent quotient": is self-aware and self-disciplined, persistent, and empathetic (Goleman, 1995)**

Ideal Component 2: An Observable Programmatic Approach to Training

In too many libraries, the training budget is woefully anemic, showing little appreciation for the time it takes to acquire new skills. In such libraries, a staff member is considered trained after attending a workshop. Attendance at 99% of the library's training programs offered is voluntary, and training programs are announced in an ad hoc manner, as isolated events unrelated to any other goings-on in the library. Below are described the fundamentals of a programmatic approach to training. For detailed checklists of the elements that comprise such an approach, see *The Trainer's Support Handbook* (Barbazette, 2001).

A long-range training schedule is evident

For training to be taken seriously by all parties, there needs to be a systematic focus on fostering continued staff competence in areas that meet the library's goals and standards. A key yardstick of the importance that a library places on training is the presence of a long-range training schedule that is well planned and well publicized. Such a schedule enables supervisors to plan ahead and informs staff about where the library is placing its energies.

The individual training events that are planned should fall into one of the following four growth tracks:

- **Technical skills building** — **Measurable, coachable**
- **Performance (or "soft") skills building** — **Observable, coachable**
- **Perspectives development** — **Enlightening, enlarges the context of the work environment**
- **Research skills development** — **Enables contributions to new knowledge**

Figure A5–1 on the next page gives examples of training events that fall within these growth tracks. For more ideas about specific training programs that promote staff growth in one of these tracks, see the chapter "How to Get Started" in *Staff Development: A Practical Guide* (Lipow, 2001).

Every training event consists of three players who have duties in three time zones

For training to be successful, there needs to be library-wide agreement that training involves more than the event itself and more than the trainee. Specifically, in relation to any training event (such as a workshop, lecture, or field trip), there are three time zones: Before, During, and After. Also, in addition to the trainee, two other players contribute to the success of training: the trainee's supervisor or the library administration, and the trainer. All three players

Figure A5–1 Examples of training events in each of four growth tracks

Growth Track	Examples of training event
Technical skills building	How to search a database Knowledge of reference tools How to manipulate virtual reference software
Performance (or "soft") skills	Question-handling techniques Dealing with difficult clients Working in a team environment
Perspectives development	Emerging technologies How others do it
Research skills development	How to conduct usability studies Survey research methods

have responsibilities in all three time zones. Figure A5–2 (pages 184 to 185) shows the responsibilities of each player in each of the time zones.

The trainers demonstrate quality teaching skills

Every trainer is not only competent in the skills being taught but also in the techniques of quality training. For example, recognizing that trainees have different ways of learning, the trainer teaches to those different ways. Also, understanding that people learn best when they are actively involved in the learning process, the trainer plans exercises in which the learner uses different senses (that is, the learner uses ears, eyes, touch, and movement to hear, talk, view, read, write, and do).

Figure A5–3, Edgar Dale's "Cone of Experience," on page 183 shows the relative effectiveness of teaching techniques that require the learner to use different senses and combinations of senses. The basic message of this diagram for a trainer is this: The more senses the learner uses, the more the learner will remember.

Ideal Component 3: A Training Plan for Every Employee

Think about when you were new on the job. If there was no formal training program to rapidly integrate you into your new workplace, it is likely you spent a lot of time feeling ignorant and uncomfortable. Perhaps you faked your way through times when you thought

Figure A5–3 **How people learn**

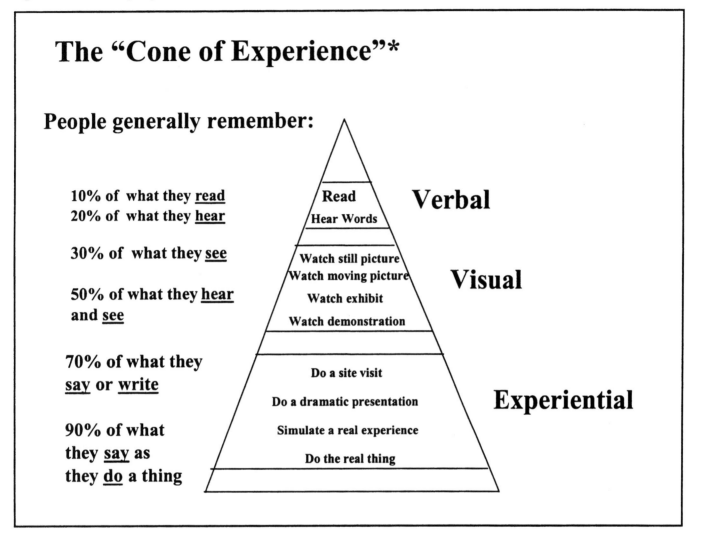

*Diagram reproduced from U.S. Department of Health and Human Services, National Drug Abuse Center for Training and Resource Development, *Training of Trainers—Trainer Manual*, page 28 [no date given].

others were expecting you to know things a new employee couldn't possibly have known. Maybe there was a time you guessed wrong and appeared not to be able to follow simple instructions or grasp an obvious concept. The following outline describes an environment that greatly reduces such awkward and misleading occurrences and brings the new employee quickly up to snuff and able to contribute fresh ideas from a standpoint of strength.

Figure A5–2 Who needs to do what, and when, to support a particular training activity

BEFORE THE TRAINING EVENT

Organization, Manager, or Supervisor
1. Determine need as it relates to the library's goals.
2. Discuss with trainer possible outcomes.
3. Decide whether attendance should be required or voluntary.
4. Brief trainee(s) on importance of this training and what to expect.
5. Discuss with trainee your expectations: new level of performance, impact on the library.
6. Relieve trainee of regular assignments.
7. Establish criteria to know when training is over.

Trainer
1. Design appropriate program.
2. Accurately describe the program in publicity.
3. Provide pre program warmup assignment.
4. Plan postprogram practice assignment.
5. Plan to teach to a variety of learning styles.
6. Prepare well-designed handouts.
7. Prepare two evaluation forms: one immediately following the program, one two weeks later to check on follow-up practice.

Trainee
1. Articulate relevance of training event to own development.
2. Discuss with supervisor postprogram expectations.
3. Plan with supervisor how to deal with regular work that won't get done while learning is in progress.

DURING THE TRAINING EVENT

Organization, Manager, or Supervisor
1. Protect trainee(s) from work-related interruptions.
2. Verify trainee(s)' attendance.

Trainer
1. Begin with "What you will learn" and why.
2. Use a variety of training technologies.
3. Teach to as many senses as possible.
4. Simulate or discuss real work environment to increase relevance.
5. Encourage two-way communication.
6. Give trainee immediate feedback as new learning is applied.
7. Distribute well-designed handouts.
8. End program with trainee(s)' planning their follow-up.

Trainee
1. Participate in exercises and discussions.
2. Take good notes.
3. Develop a plan of follow-up actions to ensure that what was learned is used on the job.
4. Identify potential barriers to applying what you learned and think of ways to overcome them.
5. Choose a "buddy" for postsession coaching back on the job.

Figure A5–2 (continued)

AFTER THE TRAINING EVENT

Organization, Manager, or Supervisor
1. Establish continued learning environment in which it is OK to make mistakes; temporarily reduce job assignments.
2. Meet immediately after training event to discuss what happened, trainee(s)' assessment, and how new knowledge will be applied, and to agree on benchmarks that will demonstrate progress in and completion of learning.
3. Inform (congratulate) trainee(s) when training is complete.

Trainer
1. Remain available to trainee(s) for follow-up consultations.
2. Send to trainee(s) a second evaluation form two weeks after event to obtain their more considered assessments and to determine how well what you taught stuck.
3. Amend your training program or techniques to achieve improvements as indicated in trainees' evaluations.
4. Based on what you learned, suggest to supervisor other programs (more advanced, more basic, on related topics).

Trainee
1. Immediately review notes and handouts.
2. Follow plans for postevent learning.
3. Work with a coach who provides feedback as you practice.
4. Regularly assess your performance to estimate what's left to practice.
5. Regard criticism of your mistakes as opportunities to improve.
6. Congratulate yourself when you have successfully completed training.

For every new job opening there is a training plan, written before the job is posted

- A training plan awaits every new employee, regardless of job title. This includes the new library director and other administrators, new librarians, new library technicians, and all new personnel who support the functioning of the building, such as those who handle building maintenance, mail distribution, and accounting.

    A training plan gives new staff a sense that their work is important. Also, because their training plan is distributed to relevant staff, trainees know that other staff are aware of their responsibilities and the schedule of training, which further contributes to that sense of importance.

- The training plan is discarded when the incumbent leaves, and a new training plan is written for the replacement. This ensures a process of rethinking the job based on the changing needs of the department or library.

- The training program has a beginning, middle, and end, with job components specified and the time estimated for the completion of training. The training plan includes as many components of the job as you can think of, as well as yardsticks for knowing when training has ended for each component. Because the focus of the training plan is the position and not the trainee, the estimated time to complete any part of the plan will vary according to the experience that the trainee brings to the job. A frequent mistake in the preparation of a training plan is to leave out a component or skill for the trainee who has had prior related experience, on the assumption that this person must already know what you have to tell him. Don't leave out anything, and to the extent that your assumption is true, the trainee will breeze through those segments of the plan. In most cases, your environment has differences that the trainee needs to know about. When training has ended, the staff member works independently.

- A draft of the training plan is distributed for suggested revisions by relevant others, who often suggest themselves as the trainer. See Figure A5–4 for a sample outline of a training plan. Notice the "Trainer" column. That is intended to remind you, and those to whom you distribute a draft plan, that the supervisor of the position need not be the trainer, and that for different responsibilities, different people throughout the library and beyond may be the appropriate ones to help with

Figure A5–4 Sample categories of a training plan

Position Title:						
Major Responsibilities	Job Duties and Tasks	Training Checklist	Trainer	Support Materials	Target Dates	Training Completed Criteria

Figure A5–5 Snippets from a sample training plan

Position Title: Reference Librarian						
Major Responsibilities	Job Duties and Tasks	Training Checklist	Trainer	Support Materials	Target Dates	Training Completed Criteria
Virtual Ref Desk	Work the desk	Handle incoming calls Schedule Software skills interviewing techniques What goes wrong?	Lucy	Software manual, VRD policies	1–2 weeks	When you feel comfortable...
		Who uses the service	Lucy			
		Browser skills	Carlos	IFP docs		
		Searching skills	Carlos			
	Analyze transaction logs	Look for threads	Vanessa	Archives of logs		
	Contribute to improving service	Suggest ways to prevent or reduce categories of questions		Examples of changes that reduced questions		

Figure A5–6 Categories to consider when planning the interview of applicants

Job Analysis		Predetermined Selection Criteria	
Duties and tasks	Skills, knowledge, experience, abilities	Selection Criteria (experience, training, and education; demonstrated skills, knowledge, and abilities)	Questions

Figure A5–7 Snippets from an interview-for-hiring plan

POSITION: Reference Librarian Job Analysis		Predetermined Selection Criteria	
Duties and tasks	Skills, knowledge, experience, abilities	Selection Criteria (experience, training, and education; demonstrated skills, knowledge, and abilities)	Questions
Work the virtual reference desk	Internet searching skills	Evidence of experience required Evidence of training desirable	Describe your experience using the Internet for reference

What special training have you had in Internet searching skills? VR skills? |
| | Public service skills | Experience working with public in a service capacity | Describe a time when you handled a difficult patron, and a time when your response didn't work so well. What would you do differently? |
| | Openness to improving the service | Experience initiating a change | Tell me about a time when you had an idea about improving an existing practice. |

the training. Through this process, the trainee is gaining new knowledge and skills that others in the trainee's unit may be unaware of.

- The final version of the plan is widely distributed to give a sense to others of the knowledge or skills to expect or not expect of the trainee over the training period. In this environment, a trainee in a top-level public library position would likely be approached not with "I suggest you call Jo Garcia and ask her if you can see the FLDC report before it is published" but with "Have you yet met with Garcia in the mayor's office?" or "I know you haven't yet been briefed on the citywide project to amalgamate certain community services, but let me say a little bit about that so you won't be completely in the dark about what's happening at the meeting we're going to."

Figure A5–5 contains snippets from a hypothetical training plan. Notice that the library's expectation that the trainee will contribute to the ever improving library environment is built into the training plan. The subtle message: All staff members know that they will be appreciated if they identify a problem, whether they or someone else caused it, and that they will be celebrated if they can suggest a solution.

The Training Plan Is the Basis for Hiring

Now that you have built a key library value—employees' contributions to change—into the training plan, you must also build that value into the hiring process. Here's the way that works:

Once the training plan is complete, the skills and experience required to perform the duties of the job as listed in the training plan are considered, and appropriate questions to ask in an oral interview are formulated. Figure A5–6 show the broad categories to consider when analyzing the position in preparation for the interview of applicants.

Then, when you fill in the blanks, be sure to include under skills, knowledge, experience, and abilities your expectations about contributions to change and devise corresponding questions that elicit relevant information. For example, in Figure A5–7, notice how this expectation is expressed ("openness to improving the service") and the candidate's related experience elicited.

Completing the Circle: Include "Contributions to Change" in Library Job Ads

In a mature learning organization, training for change goes better because you hired people who had the relevant personality characteristics and critical thinking skills. And the pool of candidates reflected these characteristics and skills because you specified them in your job ad. For example, in your blurb publicizing the position opening for a reference librarian, you might include the following in the enumeration of duties: *Shares with other staff in the delivery of virtual reference service and in the responsibility for continuous improvement of this service. And under desirable qualifications: Enjoys solving problems; is comfortable in a frequently changing work environment.*

Start Anywhere

In sum, this section briefly describes some of the important ingredients of a learning organization. You won't be able to achieve this ideal working environment in one fell swoop. However, as you incorporate the ingredients at every opportunity, three benefits will begin to emerge: (a) staff who formerly resisted new ideas, who blocked change, now either welcome it or at least have a wait-and-see attitude; (b) a growing proportion of staff contributes early to new, constructive ideas; and (c) a critical mass of buy-in to changes occurs earlier and earlier, enabling the library to move more rapidly in its chosen new direction.

References

Barbazette, Jean. 2001. *The Trainer's Support Handbook: A Practical Guide to Managing the Administrative Details of Training.* New York: McGraw Hill.

Fister, Barbara. 2002. "Fear of Reference." *Chronicle of Higher Education* 14 (June): B20.

Goleman, Daniel. 1995. *Emotional Intelligence: Why It Can Matter More Than IQ.* New York: Bantam Books.

Lipow, Anne. 2001. How to Get Started. In *Staff Development: A Practical Guide,* edited by Elizabeth F. Avery, Terry Dahlin, and Deborah A. Carver. 3rd ed. Chicago: American Library Association.

Lipow, Anne. In press, 2003. "The Librarian Has Left the Building, but Whereto?" *Internet Reference Services Quarterly* 8, no. 1/2.

Index

About the Author

Anne Grodzins Lipow, founder and director of Library Solutions Institute and Press, is a noted speaker, author, instructor, and consultant on new library issues. Since 1993, when Anne organized the first of her popular Rethinking Reference institutes, she has been sharing her concerns about the future of libraries in general, and about reference service in particular, to ensure that libraries remain relevant in the digital age. A recipient of ALA's prestigious Mudge/ Bowker award for distinguished contributions to reference librarianship, she is recognized worldwide as "one of the leading experts on reference services" (*American Libraries,* May 2002, page 85).

On new directions in reference—including issues related to staffing, space, organizational structure, and design of new services—Anne has worked with public, academic, special, and government libraries throughout the world. Among Anne's many publications is, with Roy Tennant and John Ober, the classic Internet reference book *Crossing the Internet Threshold*. At Diablo Valley College she is an occasional instructor in "Delivering Library Services: Issues, Theories, and Techniques." Formerly, Anne was Director of Library Instructional Services at the University of California, Berkeley, Libraries. You can find out more about Anne and her work at www.library-solutions.com.